Vincent South

with other duties to comply with our
request. We leave the Luabo
tomorrow morning, and before going
deposit this in a bottle ten feet
Magnetic North from a mark cut (+)
on the beacon on the island off this
harbour — For your own private
information and that of the Admiral,
I add, that we went up the river
Shire to 16°. 2. S. Lat. in the end of
March last, and with Dr Kirk and
15. Makololo we proceeded Northward
on foot tile we had discovered
a magnificent Inland ~~Lake~~
call Shirwa — 16° 2'3" Lat - S -
V. between 35° 35' and 36° 2. Long.
It is very interesting from the report
of the natives that it is separated
from a much larger Lake called
Nyinyesi — the Stars - (evidently
the Nyanja - Nyassa &c of the maps)

(Continued on back page)

LIVINGSTONE 1873–1973

W. West lithr.

LAKE NGAMI: Discovered by Oswell, Murray & Livingstone.
From a Drawing made on the spot 1850, by the Late Alfred Ryder, Esq.

Livingstone

1873–1973

EDITED BY B. W. LLOYD

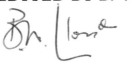

C. STRUIK (PTY) LTD, CAPE TOWN

1973

C. STRUIK (PTY) LTD
AFRICANA SPECIALISTS AND PUBLISHERS

ISBN 0 86977 027 6

PRINTED BY
GOTHIC PRINTING CO. LTD., PRINTPAK BUILDING
DACRES AVENUE, EPPING, CAPE

Contents

List of Illustrations

Preface

The ten contributions to this book are almost all the work of writers who have each devoted many years to the study of Livingstone's life. They now appear—six of them for the first time—in a Symposium to mark the Centenary of his death on 1 May, 1873. On 18 April, 1874, amid a vast congregation he was interred in Westminster Abbey. H. M. Stanley, Robert Moffat, Susi and Chuma were amongst the pallbearers.

Dr G. Seaver, who is now over 80, was to have written this preface, but replied: "I don't think I could produce anything worthwhile in 1 000 words . . . I prefer to treat him as a Spiritual adventurer against all odds. I am very glad you are doing this work for the Centenary." Those who may have read Dr Seaver's 'Life and Letters of Livingstone', 1957, will agree that it is an inspired and scholarly study, the result of many labours.

To quote from some other letters received from my contributors: First, one from Mr Quentin Keynes, whose introduction led to the happy collaboration and assistance of Mr F. R. Bradlow, of Cape Town. Mr Keynes, who is well known as broadcaster, traveller and Africana collector, says: "The B.B.C. are producing a film about Livingstone, using some scenes out of my Zambesi film. They shot many of my books by and about Livingstone (title pages, illustrations, maps etc.)". Part of one letter written from the Zambesi in 1858, which he purchased in London, led to his expedition, in search of the Baobab tree illustrated in his article, "Dr Livingstone's monogram, I presume".

Mr D. H. Varley, of Liverpool University, gave encouragement to my venture, but added with justification: "There seems to be a mass of material around relating to Livingstone, and wherever one goes, one seems to come across a batch of his letters. One sometimes wonders how much he would have written if the portable typewriter had been invented 50 years earlier."

Mr R. E. B. Sawyer, son of a long-established London bookseller, assisted me in obtaining reproductions of the medal shown on this cover. This medal was awarded to sixty of Livingstone's followers by the Royal Geographical Society in 1874. For details of these men I am grateful to Mayor F. Pridmore and Mr D. H. Simpson. Their monograph appeared in the Numismatic Circular of May, 1970, and forms a useful supplement to my "Men of Livingstone", published in 1955.

The Warden of the Scottish National Memorial Trust to David Livingstone, states: "There are several events taking place (in 1973) to commemorate the Centenary year. As always, the Trust is seeking to encourage others to make their own contributions." This Memorial is the Mecca of all who know and study Livingstone's career.

To conclude this brief introduction I quote from the inscription on the Pioneer Memorial at Mangwe Pass, Matopos, where Robert Moffat first entered Rhodesia in 1854 to establish the future Inyati Mission, which Livingstone helped to finance by a gift of £500, to his brother-in-law.

"One hundred years ago the first of the Missionaries, hunters and traders passed slowly and resolutely along this way. Honour Their Memory. They revealed to those who have followed the bounties of a country they themselves might not enjoy."

In 1954 Sir Robert Tredgold unveiled the plaque with this tribute to his ancestor's missionary zeal. (His speech is fully recorded in Rhodesiana No 1 1956.)

On May 1, 1973, Sir Robert Tredgold, in Salisbury, will present a copy of this work to a representative of the London Missionary Society in Rhodesia. It will be dedicated to the man whom the London Missionary Society released to carry the Message to the vast, unexplored regions beyond the Zambesi. The results and significance of Livingstone's labours in this Cause are now detailed in these pages. If it is true that we live on in those who come after us and that when we die we bequeath our records, Livingstone's work and words cannot but inspire posterity. In their contributions, my collaborators have all found in his records rich sources for their researches. The Symposium, as a whole, forms a planned effort to illustrate the many-sided achievements of one of history's most outstanding men.

B. W. LLOYD.

CAPE TOWN,
January, 1973.

Acknowledgement

Grateful acknowledgements are made to all the ten contributors for enabling this Centennial Symposium to be compiled; to the B.B.C. for permission to reprint Dr M. Gluckman's broadcast; to the Royal Geographical Society for the full account in their Journal of March, 1954, of the unveiling of Livingstone's Statue, Oct., 1953. The Northern Rhodesia (later Zambia) Journal gave permission to reprint its Chronology on Livingstone by Prof. J. D. Clark and G. Clay, both of whom allowed its inclusion.

I also thank the following for help and advice over this publication: Mr Vernon Brelsford; Mr E. E. Burke; Mr Quentin Keynes (for several photographs with his article); and to Mr A. Clarke for bibliographical and helpful criticism. My wife assisted the work greatly by helping to collect contributions and type correspondence. I also have to thank Miss MacMahon for typing; and Mrs M. Maytham Kidd for assistance in manuscript reading.

Two Rhodesian organisations, Anglo-American Corporation (Salisbury) and the Bata Shoe Company, Gwelo, have given financial aid. Mr F. R. Bradlow gave generously of his time in his most original contribution involving much research into a subject hitherto completely overlooked. Messrs C. Struik (Pty) Ltd undertook publication as a timely and enduring memorial to Dr Livingstone's immortal career.

The Livingstone Legend

REV. G. OWEN LLOYD

The lionizing of Livingstone was a fashion in British missionary circles for many years. Mission hospitals, churches, halls, hostels, streets, squares and towns all bear his name. The memory of his personality seems to have been overwhelmed by the propaganda value of his name. It was most refreshing to hear a living missionary tell recently that he had read in the minutes of some missionary meeting how Livingstone was being hauled over the coals for leaving his mission station and trekking all over the countryside instead of getting on with the task of evangelising the local people. A motion of censure had been proposed and seconded in this meeting of missionaries at which Livingstone was present. When the censors had had their say, one of the Moffats proposed a counter-motion approving of Livingstone's actions. According to the minutes of the meeting, Livingstone seconded the counter-motion himself!

It is still a matter of debate whether Livingstone was a missionary who travelled widely preparing the way for other missionaries or whether he was a traveller who started as a missionary and ended up being an explorer. This argument may never be settled but it is important to remember what was expected of a missionary in the middle of the nineteenth century in Africa. Health risks for himself and his family,

1

problems of language and communication, maintenance of supplies, primitive wars and the mental task of keeping a balanced sense of values were obvious difficulties. But perhaps the most difficult problem for the missionary was his task of being an agent for a society thousands of miles away across the sea in a country where Karl Marx published the Communist Manifesto in 1848 and Charles Darwin's "Origin of Species" appeared in 1859. If a missionary is an agent of a society living in a particular country at a particular time, then David Livingstone was a missionary. Indeed, he made the claim himself in a letter to his father written in 1850. In the letter he rejected an offer to join his brother Charles in America with the words: "I am a missionary, heart and soul."

It was as a missionary—commissioned by the London Missionary Society—that in March, 1841, he stepped ashore at Simon's Town, near Cape Town, a man of twenty-seven years of age. His preparation for thirty years of life in the parts of Africa unknown to the British people had been an upbringing in a poor but Christian home in Scotland, work in a cotton mill from the age of ten, education at night school for two hours a night for thirteen years, four years of medical training and some theological study at an Independent seminary. The fascination of the gipsy life of travel in Africa in a tented wagon drawn by oxen gripped him and his natural talent for observation soon showed in his letters and reports. For more than a quarter of a century his sturdy physique endured the rigours of this open-air existence and he survived the attacks of fever, the unhealthy water supplies, the extremes of temperature and the many hours of travel in scorching sun and soaking rain.

A biographer of David Livingstone has divided his thirty years in Africa into five main periods. The first eleven years of *missionary apprenticeship* were spent in following the example

2

of his peers in the mission field. By 1852 he was a family man with four children, having married Mary Moffat. These members of his family he loved too much to expose them to the risks of life in Central Africa. Having sent them to Britain, he became the *traveller* who trekked across Central Africa from west to east. Journeying light by canoe, or on the back of an ox, or on foot, this three-year trek was perhaps his finest hour. His reports made him the popular hero of Victorian England. But he paid the price of this hero-worship in the next period of *expedition* when he was appointed to explore the Zambesi. The high moments and failures of this expedition are fully recorded and by the end of the expedition he was a man of fifty years. What he had seen of the slave trade had challenged him to go back as a *liberator* and tackle the slave trade at its sources of supply. It was a one-man fight. So it was as a lonely *pilgrim* that H. M. Stanley found him at Ujiji in November, 1871, some sixteen months before his heart was left in Africa.

When David Livingstone arrived at the southern end of Africa the maps of the time were interested in mountains, deserts and rivers, and in this respect the map of Africa was based more on conjecture than on scientific observation. The centre of the continent of Africa was usually decorated with sketches of weird wild animals. Christian missions had not moved southwards from Ethiopia or crossed the Sahara desert. Nor had mission endeavour moved inland from the coast line of West Africa. In the south missions had been confined to those parts that were settled and where ministers of religion from other continents and their families could survive as witnesses and teachers of the Christian way of life. For the people of the North Atlantic continents, Central Africa was an area of mystery and misery.

Into that part of Africa occupied by the Bakwena tribe Livingstone went as a missionary in company with Rogers

Edwards. After an exploratory trip he returned in 1842, ready to learn the language and erect buildings. Tribal troubles frustrated their efforts, but by the following year they had established a station at Mabotsa among the BaKgatla. Personality clashes of the kind that made Pearl Buck entitle her book on missionaries in China "Fallen Angels", resulted in Livingstone moving to the village of Tshonwane, that Sechele had built for the Bakwena tribe. But the village was badly situated for water supplies and Livingstone, who had by then acquired the water consciousness of Africa, persuaded him to move ten miles to Dimawe. This was the village that was attacked by the Boers while Livingstone was on one of his journeys. On his travels he met the MaKololo tribe living in the malaria-ridden Chobe swamps and planned for them to move to the Batoka highlands between the Zambesi and the Kafue. If establishing mission stations is the test of the success of a missionary, then it can be said fairly that Livingstone made a noble attempt in those early years to persuade the tribes he met to settle at healthy and accessible places.

A closer look at his work on one of these stations can be taken by referring to some of his letters. In one he tells how they rose at sunrise and had family worship and breakfast before school. Manual work followed in the form of ploughing, sowing and work in the smithy. Scripture classes or visiting took place before the cows had to be milked and prayers conducted by eight-thirty when everybody was ready for bed. Livingstone's comment on this routine was that it left little time for real missionary work. Like many another missionary he built his own house, fell off the roof, dug an irrigation channel and built a dam.

The greatest achievement of Livingstone, the missionary, crystallised after his death. His appeal that Africa should be freed from slavery is as strong and necessary today as it was a

Ukhonongo October 1873

Sir

We have heared in the month of August that you have started from Zanzibar for Unyenyembe, and again and again lately we have heared your arrivel. your father died by disease beyond the country of Bisa, but we have carried the corpse with us. 10 of our soldier are lost and some have died. Our han presses us to ask you some clothes to buy provision for our soldiers. and we should have an answer that when we shall enter there shall be firing guns or not, and if you permit us to fire guns, then send some powder We have wrote these few words in the place of Sultan or king Mbowra.

The writer Jacob Wainright
Dr Livingstone Exped

Letter from Jacob Wainwright reporting the death of David Livingstone, October, 1873.

Discovery of Lake Ngami, 1 August, 1849.

century ago. Mental and spiritual enslavement is nothing new but the inspiration to strive for freedom from enslavement of all kinds still arises from the sight of the statue of Livingstone above the Devil's Cataract at the Victoria Falls.

The inspiration of Livingstone led to men and women pioneering their Christian way into Central Africa, and living and dying there for the sake of the Gospel of salvation through Jesus Christ. His concern that the resources of land, people and water should be used as gifts from God gave rise to dreams and plans about navigable rivers and continental trade. Not only was Central Africa opened for the interest of people of other continents, the people of Africa were also shaken out of their tribal isolation by contact with a man who could speak to them about other people like themselves. Ten years after he had passed through the Rovuma valley, an African to whom he had given a coat, remembered him as "a short man with a bushy moustache and a keen, piercing eye, whose words were always gentle and whose manners were always kind, and who knew the way to the hearts of all men". That description does not apply to David Livingstone, the explorer, or to Livingstone, leader of a trans-Africa expedition, or to Livingstone, the liberator of the slaves. It can only be a tribute from Africa to David Livingstone, the Missionary.

The Variants of the 1857 edition of Livingstone's Missionary Travels and Researches in South Africa

FRANK R. BRADLOW

John Carter, in his book *ABC for Book Collectors*, defines a "variant" of an edition as "a general-purpose term used to describe a copy or copies of an EDITION exhibiting some variation, whether of text, title-page, illustrations, paper or binding from another copy or copies of the same edition. Its use does not necessarily imply that the copy or copies are abnormal; in fact it is most frequently and properly used when doubt exists as to the priority, or even the precise relationship, between the two or more observed variants and where in consequence no norm has been established. As Greg once put it: 'I have treated bibliographical variants as essentially unordered'."

Carter remarks further, that he considers it "imprudent to talk about earliest issues", considering it better to refer to "variants of . . . an issue", or of an edition.[1]

This definition of Carter's is not only very relevant to a discussion of the differences between various copies of the 1857 edition of Livingstone's *Missionary Travels and Researches in South Africa*, published by John Murray, but, because of the doubts that exist about the "precise relationship of the observed" copies of the book, it also aptly sums up

6

the problems confronting a bibliographer in considering these variants.†

My attention was first drawn to the differences between various copies of this edition by Mr John Maggs, of Maggs Bros. Limited, the antiquarian booksellers of Berkeley Square, London. Mr Maggs pointed out to me that in some copies of the 1857 edition there was an extra leaf consisting of two pages numbered 8* on the recto and 8+ on the verso. This extra leaf, which has been tipped-in, consists for the most part of an extensive interpolation, giving a description of Moffat's mission at Kuruman, and Livingstone's courtship of, and marriage to, Mary Moffat. In the copies with this extra leaf a large portion of the original page 8 has been altered. In the copies which do not have the extra leaf, lines 9, 10, 11, 12, 13 and 14 of page 8 read as follows: "Spending but a short time there [Cape Town] I started for the interior by going round to Algoa Bay, and soon proceeded inland, and have spent the following sixteen years of my life, namely from 1840 to 1856, in medical and missionary labours there without cost to the inhabitants." The remainder of the page is devoted to an

†The title-page in all the variant issues of this edition is the same, and reads as follows:
MISSIONARY TRAVELS / and / RESEARCHES IN SOUTH AFRICA / including a sketch of / sixteen years residence in the interior of Africa / and a journey from the Cape of Good Hope to Loanda on the West / Coast; thence across the continent, down the River / Zambesi, to the Eastern Ocean. / BY DAVID LIVINGSTONE, LL.D. D.C.L., / Fellow of the Faculty of Physicians and Surgeons, Glasgow; corresponding member of the / Geographical and Statistical Society of New York; Gold medallist and corresponding / member of the Royal Geographical Societies of London and Paris / F.S.A., Etc. Etc. / woodcut engraving of insect / *TSETSE Fly—Magnified*—See page 571 / with portrait, maps by Arrowsmith, and numerous illustrations. / London: / JOHN MURRAY, ALBEMARLE STREET / 1857. / *The right of Translation is reserved.*

apology for his lack of "those literary qualifications which are acquired by habits of writing".

In the variants with the extra leaf, however, although the wording of page 8 is identical for the first ten lines, a change occurs in the eleventh line. The passage now reads: "Spending but a short time there, I started for the interior by going to Algoa Bay, and soon proceeded inland *to the mission station in the Bechuana country called Kuruman, which is about seven hundred miles from Cape Town.*" The change it will be noticed, occurs with the insertion of the passage in italics. Most of the rest of the page is then devoted to a description of Kuruman. Livingstone, in a rare moment of Victorian sentimentality then relates how "he screwed up courage to put a question beneath one of the fruit-trees which, I believe, is generally accompanied by a thrilling sensation in the bosom, and which those who have never felt it can no more explain than the blind man who thought that scarlet colour was like the sound of a trumpet . . ." After this brief admission, most of page 8* is devoted to a brief account of his married life and the upbringing of their children. Page 8+ is almost entirely devoted to the same apology, in identical words, for his "lack of literary qualifications" that appears on page 8 of the obviously earlier issue. The reference to the "obviously earlier issue", is because it would seem apparent that the extra leaf had been "tipped-in" later to provide for the interpolation, otherwise the pagination would have been normal and would not have required the same page number differentiated only by "asterisks" and "plus" signs.

Greatly intrigued by this particular variant of the 1857 edition, I compared the two copies of *Missionary Travels and Researches*, in my own collection, with those in the various collections of the South African Library, Cape Town, and with two copies in the Strange Collection of the Johannesburg

Public Library. Discussing the problem with Mrs Thea Smit who is in charge of the Mendelssohn Revision Project, I discovered that this extra leaf was not by any means the only difference between various copies of the 1857 edition, but that there were, in addition, variations in illustrations, list of illustrations, and index as well.

Correspondence by me with Mr Robin Fryde of Frank R. Thorold (Pty) Limited; with Mr B. W. Lloyd of Salisbury; and with various South African libraries and archives, enabled me, with Mrs Smit's invaluable assistance, to distinguish clearly at least nine definite variants of this first edition of *Missionary Travels and Researches* . . .

Only variations in the extra leaf, the illustrations, the "List of Illustrations", and the index have been considered in this article. Questions of differences in bindings and paper have not been examined as this would have complicated the matter still further.

Copies of *Missionary Travels and Researches* . . . in the major South African institutions had already been examined in the course of the Mendelssohn Revision Project. Further correspondence by me with a few libraries and three antiquarian booksellers meant that, in all, no less than thirty-three institutions, private collectors and booksellers provided information about this book and its variants. These institutions and collections were made up of twenty-seven libraries, archives and universities in the Republic of South Africa; the National Archives of Rhodesia; two private collections, and three antiquarian booksellers. Several of these institutions and collections possess more than one copy of the book so that a wide field has been covered. This exhaustive research has not only yielded, as has been said, nine clearly defined variants, but possibly at least two more.

The greatest variation is in the nature—not the quantity—

of the illustrations, as will be seen. In his catalogue No. 94 of 1969, Gaston Renard, bookseller, lists three variants. The first item he lists as "the first issue of the first edition". He describes it as follows:

"Portrait. Two folding maps by Arrowsmith. Two tinted lithographic plates; one black and white lithograph, plus 41 wood-cut illustrations (including 20 full-page) 8pp original adverts dated Nov. 1, 1857 at end."

"The lithographs; folding frontispiece Victoria Falls; plate at p. 66, 'Lake Ngami . . .'; plate at p. 225, 'Bechuana reeddance . . .'; the first two of which are tinted, are *lithographed by* W. West, the third is from a sketch by Bell."

He then lists as the "second issue of the first edition" the same book, but a copy where "all three plates have been redrawn". "*The lithographs were done by T. Picken and printed by Day and Son*, and all three plates are tinted."

As the "third issue of the first edition", he lists a copy that is identical in all respects to the previous two copies, save and except that "these three plates are identical in design to those of the second issue, but have been re-done as woodcuts by J. W. Whymper and the 'Bechuana reed-dance . . .' is from a sketch by Ford . . ."

"The third issue has an extra leaf following page 8, numbered 8* and 8+ with signature B3 at the foot. This tipped-in leaf was necessitated by Livingstone's revision and extension of the two final paragraphs of the Introductory chapter."

Whether Renard is correct in describing the variant with the two tinted lithographs by W. West as the "first issue" is not yet proved. The only thing that can be said with certainty is that the issue with the extra leaf numbered 8* and 8+, is *not* the first issue. To show how opinions can vary on the order of precedence of the variant issues, it is sufficient to state that Frank R. Thorold (Pty) Limited in their Catalogue

10

No. 5, New Series 1973,[2] in fact describe Gaston Renard's "second issue"—the one with the three lithographs by T. Picken—as the first issue.

However for the purpose of this article Gaston Renard's order of issue has been retained in the table given below, showing the variants. This is not because of a belief in its correctness but merely for convenience.

It will be noticed that the engraved portrait of Livingstone, the title-page, the colophon, maps, advertisements, and all the plates except the frontispiece, and those opposite pages 66 and 225, appear to be the same in all the variants. The other 41 illustrations are all wood-cuts by J. W. Whymper. Twelve of the original sketches were by the well-known animal painter Joseph Wolf. A. H. Palmer in his book *The Life of Joseph Wolf, Animal Painter*[3] considers that the illustrations were a failure. He describes *Missionary Travels and Researches . . .* "as a book defaced rather than illustrated by a number of wood-cuts so atrociously engraved, and for the most part so utterly wanting in good qualities, that it is very small praise to pronounce the twelve by Wolf the best of them.[3]" He gives Wolf's pictures as those facing pages 13, 26, 27, 56, 71, 140, 142, 210, 242, 498, 562 and 588. These wood-cuts are sometimes incorrectly described as steel engravings.[4]

The plate opposite p. 66 entitled "Lake Ngami, discovered by Oswell, Murray and Livingstone", is described in Picken's tinted lithograph, Whymper's wood-cut, and West's four-colour chromolithograph, as being "from a Drawing made on the spot (1850) by the late Alfred Ryder Esq." It is puzzling therefore to find that in West's chromolithograph the illustration has been so altered as to omit the standing figure of Dr Livingstone himself, although his wife and children remain in the picture (see coloured frontispiece). This is, as far as I am aware, an unexplained bibliographical mystery, especially as

11

the original water-colour in the Library of Parliament, Cape Town, does show Livingstone as in Picken's and Whymper's prints. (See Variant No. 6.)

It will also be noticed from the table on p. 16 that only one issue, Variant No. 8, contains the index. In order to simplify the comparison of the different issues the variants are presented in a tabular form, originated by Mrs Thea Smit, but greatly altered by the writer who is solely responsible for all errors.

VARIANT NO. 9

It has been pointed out by Mrs D. W. Fold of the Cory Library for Historical Research, Rhodes University, Grahamstown, that there is yet another variant, which contains an error in the "List of Illustrations". As it has not been possible to examine all copies, I quote from her letter: "In the 'List of Illustrations', illustration No. 16 is given as 'Bechuana Reed-Dance by Moonlight . . . 225,' and illustration No. 17 as 'A new or striped variety of Eland found north of Sesheke . . . 210.' In our other two copies the correct page order is maintained, i.e. No. 16 is given as, 'A new or striped variety of Eland, found north of Sesheke . . . 210,' and No. 17 as "Bechuana Reed-Dance by Moonlight . . . 225." On examining the two copies in my own collection, I find a similar situation. In my copy of Variant No. 2, the incorrect page order for illustrations No. 16 and 17 is given in the "List of Illustrations", as quoted by Mrs Fold, while in my copy of Variant No. 3 these two plates are found in the correct page order in the "List of Illustrations".

POSSIBLE VARIANTS NO. 10 AND 11

To add to the complexity of the subject there would appear to be one, and possibly two, other variants in the stocks held by the antiquarian booksellers, Maggs Bros. Limited, in London. In a letter received by me from Mr John Maggs in November, 1972, referring to the variants of *Missionary Travels and Researches* . . ., he writes as follows: "We have now checked twenty-three copies. Of seven of these which had the extra page 8, six have uncoloured engraved frontispieces (*Variant No. 3. Note by FRB*) and one has an uncoloured lithographed frontispiece (*A tenth variant?*) (*Note by FRB.*) Of sixteen copies without the extra page 8, eleven have uncoloured engraved frontispieces, two have uncoloured lithographed frontispieces, and three have coloured lithographed frontispieces. *In the two with uncoloured lithographed frontispieces, the frontispiece and plate at page 225 are by Davy,* but in the three with coloured lithographed frontispieces they are by West." (Italics mine FRB.) Mr Maggs adds, "I think it would deserve much further study." His letter is the first reference to a copy of a variant with the extra leaf having a *lithographic* frontispiece. All other copies of Variant No. 3 with the extra leaf are shown as having the frontispiece and illustrations opposite pages 66 and 225, done in black and white wood-cut. The copy mentioned by Mr Maggs would therefore certainly constitute a tenth variant, but it has not been possible to include it in the comparison table above in the absence of further details.

It would also appear that the two copies, he mentions, with uncoloured lithographic frontispieces and plate at page 225, could be a further variant, but here again more detailed information is necessary. This is possibly an eleventh variant as the name of Davy as a lithographer of these, or any plates, is not mentioned in the information given by South African institutions and collectors. It is presumed that Mr Maggs is referring to tinted lithographs, when he describes the lithographed plates as "uncoloured", (as opposed to coloured lithographs done by chromolithography).

TABLE SHOWING VARIANTS OF LIVINGSTONE'S MISSIONARY TRAVELS AND RESEARCHES IN SOUTH AFRICA, 1857 EDITION*

Variant No.	Frontispiece	Plate opposite p. 66	Plate opposite p. 255	Extra Leaf or Index	Date of Presentation Inscription	Location
1	Tinted lithograph by West	Tinted lithograph by West	Black and white lithograph from sketch by Bell			CS CU DU DUK GP GU JA PS PU SU
2	Tinted lithograph by T. Picken, printed by Day & Son	Tinted lithograph by T. Picken, printed by Day & Son	Tinted lithograph by T. Picken, printed by Day & Son		29.10.1857 26.10.1857 29.10.1857	BPL CBR CS (GC) DP DUK GM JOP JP JTH JU KP PFP

No.						Location
3	Black and white wood-cut by J. W. Whymper	Black and white wood-cut by J. W. Whymper	Black and white wood-cut by J. W. Whymper	Yes. Extra leaf; pages 8* and 8+	28. 2.1858	CBR CLP CS (FC) DP JH JOP JTH PUS SU
4	Tinted lithograph by T. Picken, printed by Day & Son	Wood-cut by J. W. Whymper	Wood-cut by J. W. Whymper		2.11.1857	CS JP JU PEU
5	Tinted lithograph by T. Picken, printed by Day & Son	(a) Tinted lithograph by T. Picken, printed by Day & Son (b) Tinted lithograph by W. West	(a) Tinted lithograph by T. Picken, printed by Day & Son (b) Tinted lithograph by W. West			CLP

It will be noted that this variant has the three lithographs by T. Picken as in No. 2, plus the two by West shown as (b) at pages 66 and 225

*For the meaning of abbreviations given in column 7, "Location", see list at end of this article.

15

Variant No.	Frontispiece	Plate opposite p. 66	Plate opposite p. 255	Extra Leaf or Index	Date of Presentation Inscription	Location
6	Chromolithograph in four colours by W. West	Chromolithograph in four colours by W. West	Chromolithograph in four colours by W. West			JH RNA RL
7	Black and white wood-cut by J. W. Whymper	Black and white wood-cut by J. W. Whymper	Black and white wood-cut by J. W. Whymper			BUO DU GU JTH PA PEDW PMA PMU
	Note: The difference between this variant and Variant No. 3, is that there is no extra leaf after page 8					
8	Black and white wood-cut by J. W. Whymper	Black and white wood-cut by J. W. Whymper	Black and white wood-cut by J. W. Whymper	This variant has an index, starting after a blank page 688, on page 689 (un-numbered) and ending on page 711		CU GU JOP KP RNA

16

This study of the variants of the 1857 edition of Livingstone's *Missionary Travels and Researches in South Africa* does not pretend to be exhaustive. There are, doubtless, several other possible variants which bibliographers will distinguish in the course of time. When Miss M. E. Appleyard compiled her bibliography, *Dr David Livingstone*[5] in 1949, she listed only three of the variants mentioned in this study, viz. Nos. 3, 6 and 8, and it took many years for researchers to extend this list. In fact it can be clearly said that were it not for the devoted researches of Mrs Thea Smit and her colleagues in the Mendelssohn Revision Project much of the new information would not have been uncovered. Sidney Mendelssohn's *South African Bibliography*[6] published in 1910, makes no mention of any variants at all.

Even this detailed study suggests no answer to the question of, in what order were the variants issued? The only thing the tabulated comparison would seem to show is that Variant No. 2, with the three tinted lithographs by T. Picken which were printed by Day and Son, is the one that occurs most frequently in the copies examined. It is found in sixteen of the thirty-two collections from which information was obtained.

Mr Robin Fryde of Frank R. Thorold (Pty) Limited, in a letter dated 15.9.1972 asks pertinently: "All these copies have the November 1st 1857 advert of John Murray. Why are so few copies found with the index? And what of the coloured copies?" It might also be asked why the publisher replaced the wood-cuts with Picken's lithographs, and Picken's lithographs with West's, and in what order he did this? Was the standing figure of Livingstone in the chromolithograph of "Lake Ngami . . ." opposite page 66 omitted at Livingstone's request, and if so, why? Also, why did Livingstone decide to have the extra leaf after page 8 inserted? Did he feel he had neglected his wife by not mentioning her in this way in the first place? All these questions and a host of others will occur to trained bibliographers and it may well be, that, in the future, some indefatigable researcher will find some of the answers. What is certain is that this important book should not be considered as a mere bibliographical curiosity. In this year, 1973, the centenary of Livingstone's death, it retains its position as one of the important, perceptive, and enthralling books of African travel and exploration.

ACKNOWLEDGEMENTS

I would like to acknowledge my indebtedness to Mrs Thea Smit (my constant mentor), Mr John Maggs, Mr Robin Fryde, Mr C. Lloyd of the Grahamstown Public Library, Mrs P. W. Fold of the Cory Library, Mr F. J. Potgieter of the Library of the University of the Orange Free State, Mr P. J. van der Walt of the Bloemfontein Public Library, Mr G. J. Reynecke of the Government Archives, Pretoria, and Mr B. W. Lloyd of Salisbury.

NOTES AND REFERENCES

1. Carter, J., *ABC for Book Collectors*. Rupert Hart-Davis, London 1972, p. 204.
2. Frank R. Thorold (Pty) Ltd., *Catalogue No. 5 (New Series)*, Johannesburg, 1973, Item 348.
3. Palmer, A. H., *The Life of Joseph Wolf, Animal Painter*. Longman's Green, London, 1895, p. 123.
4. Frank R. Thorold (Pty) Limited, *Catalogue No. 5 (New Series)*, Johannesburg, 1973, Item 348b.
5. Appleyard, M. E., *Dr David Livingstone. A bibliography*. University of Cape Town Libraries, Cape Town, 1970.
6. Mendelssohn, Sidney, *South African Bibliography*, 2 vols. Kegan Paul, London, 1910.

The abbreviations used in column number 7, "Locations", and their meaning.
Bloemfontein
BLP   Bloemfontein Public Library

BUO	University of Orange Free State
Cape Town	
CBR	Bradlow Collection
CLP	Library of Parliament
CS	South African Library
CS (GC)	South African Library (Grey Collection)
CS (FC)	South African Library (Fairbridge Collection)
CU	University of Cape Town
Durban	
DP	Durban Public Library
DU	University of Natal, Durban
DUK	Killie Campbell Collection, University of Natal
Grahamstown	
GM	Grahamstown Museum
GP	Grahamstown Public Library
GU	Rhodes University
Johannesburg	
JH	Humphreys Collection, University of the Witwatersrand
JOP	Oppenheimer Collection
JP	Johannesburg Public Library
JTH	Frank R. Thorold (Pty) Limited
JU	University of the Witwatersrand
Kimberley	
KP	Kimberley Public Library
Pretoria	
PA	National Archives
PEDW	Wagener Collection. Dept. of National Education
PS	State Library
PU	University of Pretoria
PUS	Van Schaik Collection, University of South Africa
Port Elizabeth	
PEP	Port Elizabeth Public Library
PEU	University of Port Elizabeth
Pietermaritzburg	
PMA	National Archives
PMU	University of Natal, Pietermaritzburg
Rhodesia	
RNA	National Archives of Rhodesia, Salisbury
RL	B. W. Lloyd Collection, Salisbury
Stellenbosch	
SU	University of Stellenbosch

David Livingstone's Management of Malaria—its Historical Significance

PROF. MICHAEL GELFAND

Most people look upon David Livingstone as an explorer, geographer or a Christian missionary, who opened up new paths in Central Africa single-handed but few think of him as a medical practitioner, although this was the qualification that caused Robert Moffat to send him to his mission at Kuruman in 1841. He might not go down in the annals of history as a great physician, but had it not been for his management of attacks of malaria, he would not have survived but shared the fate of those who attempted to penetrate these unhealthy regions before him. The Zambesi Expedition of 1858–1863 would have ended in disaster were it not for Livingstone's control of the malaria.

At first Livingstone was content to practise his art for a number of years in Botswana. His practice was a rather monotonous one in which dozens of sick and well lined up for a taste of his mixtures. But that is not why he moved. He soon discovered that his ideas on the Africans were different from those of the Boers on his Eastern border and the two could not be reconciled. If he wanted to live happily and peacefully amongst the Africans and preach as he thought fit, he must go elsewhere away from contact with his Boer neighbours. He had heard of a great tribe under Sebituane who lived further

Livingstone weak from fever escorted to Shinte's Town.

The Bronze Statue erected in front of the Royal Geographical Society London, in honour of David Livingstone, unveiled October, 1953.

north in a most unhealthy fever-ridden belt 200 miles north of Lake Ngami. The mission of his dreams could not be a reality except in a healthy place and he hoped he might find one somewhere in these regions. His mission had to have easy access to the sea so that he could procure supplies for it to avoid the journey south with its threats from the Boers. His obsessional make-up would not allow him to be stopped by obstacles. He thought deeply and devised a method of treating the fever. Although he personally did not succeed in establishing his healthy mission to the north he paved the way for others by proving that with the proper use of quinine the white man could survive and so, as a result, not long after his death in 1873 Europeans found they could live in the lands of the Zambesi.

Whilst practising in Southern Botswana, Livingstone was both a hard worker and an avid reader of medical books and journals. He received regularly the *British and Foreign Medical Review* and the *Lancet* which Robert Moffat had ordered.[1]

As he was so engrossed with the fever belt beyond Lake Ngami to the north of him, it could not have been mere coincidence that he obtained a copy of the *Medical History of the Expedition to the Niger during the years 1841–2* by James Ormiston McWilliam, the Medical Officer in charge of the Expedition.[2] McWilliam mentions his medical findings which probably led to the failure of the expedition. His method of administering quinine left much to be desired for it was generally withheld until later in the course of the illness. This Livingstone must have noticed. McWilliam also gives details of the eight autopsies performed. All these patients died of malaria and he observed that in three cases the gall bladder was distended with bile, "of the colour and consistency of tar". This greatly struck Livingstone and caused him to

21

prepare his famous pill of quinine and purgatives to rid the system of bile.

He felt it was most important to find a remedy for the fever before he left for Sebituane's country. On 10 August, 1849, he visited Lake Ngami and the Zouga River to see Lechulatebe to ask for guides to accompany him to the Makololo Chief. He was prepared for any attack of fever that he might contract on this journey. He would take quinine as soon as symptoms appeared with, at the time, strong purgatives to rid the liver of its excessive thick bile. This would be followed up with big doses of quinine until the ears rang. Unfortunately he could not go beyond the Zouga River as he was not able to obtain guides. He returned to Kolobeng, where he remained until April, 1850, when he left again for Sebituane's, this time taking his wife and three children with him. On his way he heard that a party of Englishmen, who had gone to the lake in search of ivory, were all laid low with fever and one of them, Alfred Rider, had died of it. He reached Lechulatebe and arranged with him for guides to take him to Sebituane on ox-back whilst his family would wait for him at Lake Ngami. When all was ready for his departure his little boy and girl were seized with fever and the following day all the servants developed the same complaint. So he was forced to give up his plan to go to Sebituane that year. He now had the opportunity of trying out his remedy and all his patients recovered rapidly. He noticed that the fever responded immediately to quinine. He then returned to Kolobeng with his party, disappointed at not being able to go to Makololo country but glad that his remedy for fever was effective.

In 1851, when he reached Linyanti, Sebituane's capital, Livingstone was left in no doubt as to the virulence of the fever there. His attention was drawn to the fact that the majority of the people whom Sebituane had brought into these parts were much more affected by it than the indigenous or "River races",[3] the inhabitants of the country. Here he offered himself as "a forlorn hope to ascertain whether there is a place fit to be a sanatorium for more unhealthy spots".[3]

Instead of again exposing his family to these unhealthy regions, Livingstone sent them back to England before he set out on his second journey to Linyanti in 1852. Sebituane had died when he was there in 1851 so now he went to see chief Sekeletu his successor.

Although he had tried out his remedy at Lake Ngami and been satisfied with it Livingstone still appreciated that there might be a still better one which he was prepared to use if it became available. Even if it came from a witch doctor, he would have no qualms about trying it. He was a man with an open mind and respect for the ideas of others. So when he had his first attack of fever on 30 May, 1853, at Linyanti and then relapsed on 2 June, he submitted to a trial with an unorthodox remedy. He wrote, "Anxious to ascertain whether the natives possessed the knowledge of any remedy of which we were ignorant, I requested the assistance of one of Sekeletu's doctors. He put some roots into a pot with water, and when it was boiling placed it on a spot beneath blankets thrown around both me and it. This provided no immediate effect; he then got a small bundle of different kinds of medicinal woods, and burning them in a potsherd nearby to us he used the smoke and hot vapour arising from them as an auxiliary to the other in causing diaphoresis. I fondly hoped that they had a more potent remedy than our medicines afford; but after being stewed in their vapour baths, smoked like a red herring over green twigs, and charmed *secundem artem*, I concluded that I could cure the fever more quickly than they can.[4]"

Armed with his quinine and antimalarial pills, Livingstone left Linyanti in 1853, en route for the nearest coast to find out how easy it would be to reach the sea for supplies if he set up a mission in a healthy spot in these regions. He reached the west coast and then dissatisfied with that route he returned to Makololo country and from there set off for Tete and the east coast, following roughly the course of the Zambesi River. He thus crossed Africa from West to East but not without suffering severely and repeatedly from acute pyrexial bouts of malaria. However he always took his quinine and as soon as a paroxysm was over struggled on with his journey. By the time he returned to Sekeletu he was able to throw off each attack with increasing ease, owing to the resistance his body was building up to the various strains of malaria. He was becoming what was often referred to in later years as "salted". With his quinine salt and relative care he was able to overcome the malaria with utmost regularity although he still ran the risk of contracting black water fever, which, somehow, he escaped, and which was not yet realised to be a complication of malaria. He tells us on many occasions of the prescription he used. First of all he prepared the pill, which became known as the "*Livingstone Pill*". For an adult, "take resin of jalap and of calomel, of each 8 grains; of quinine and rhubarb, of each 4 grains. Mix them all together in a mortar and preserve for use. When required make the mixture into pills with the spirit of Cardamoms. Dose from 10 to 20 grains. The operation of this dose in from 4 to 6 hours removes all the violent symptoms, as racking pains in the head, back and loins, and all the bones, dry skin, thirst etc. If this time passes, a dessert spoon of salts promotes the operation. Then quinine in 4 to 6 grain doses every 2 or 3 hours till the ears ring or deafness ensues completes the one, without, in general, any loss of strength being sustained . . . with it fever is not worse than a cold!!".[5]

After this he returned to England, severed his connection with the London Missionary Society and then organised an expedition to the Zambesi to ascend it from the Victoria Falls, believing it was navigable all the way. He engaged Dr John Kirk (later Sir John) as medical officer to the expedition and took great care to ensure that his precautions against and treatment of malaria were adopted. He had, by this time, become familiar with the recently introduced regime of using quinine as a prophylactic. When Livingstone was making arrangements for his Zambesi Expedition with the Foreign Office he learned of the medical findings of the 1854 Niger Expedition under Dr William Baikie. It will be recalled how heavy was the loss of life from malaria in the 1841–2 Expedition. A naval medical officer, Alexander Bryson, had found that malaria could be prevented by serving daily amounts of quinine bark in wine to men serving in tropical climates, so in the 1854 Expedition Baikie issued prophylactic quinine to all his men. As a result the Expedition remained on the Niger River for four months without a single European death. Livingstone was confident he could cure the fever.[6] Perhaps he could prevent it; so he instructed Kirk that before they entered the Delta of the Zambesi, all Europeans were to be given two grains of quinine in sherry every day. He left no stone unturned and paid attention even to the smallest detail in order to ensure that his Expedition reached the mouth of the Zambesi in the dry, more healthy season. It arrived there on 6 May and from the 11th the men were issued each day with quinine in sherry. The health of the men was excellent at first while they were in the lower river and Commander Bedingfeld, the Naval Officer in Charge of the steam launch *Ma-Robert* appeared to be critical of the fuss Livingstone made about malaria. But at this time the weather was almost temperate. Things soon changed. When the men reached Expedition Island a few miles up the Zambesi fever appeared and at times Baines was delirious with it. Livingstone himself was beginning to doubt the value of prophylactic quinine, but no one can be certain that the men really took it as ordered, for by July Livingstone and Bedingfeld were at loggerheads. More than one factor was responsible for this, but it is interesting that one of the reasons advanced by Livingstone for their quarrel was that Bedingfeld refused to take his prophylactic quinine. On 31 July Bedingfeld resigned.

There is no doubt that the Livingstone regime saved the men and the expedition for whenever the fever appeared large amounts of quinine were given early. "Quinine," Livingstone wrote, "has a good and prompt effect in all cases if used with other remedies and in sufficient quantities. I took about 30 grains in six hours and it made me deaf soon after." By March, 1859, after a whole rainy season in the lower Zambesi, Livingstone and Kirk considered that it was time to make an official report on the African fever. They submitted a despatch on it to Sir James Clark, referring to the quinine which was taken regularly by all the Europeans with a single exception (Bedingfeld). Two grains were taken in sherry every day and the writers were disposed to attribute their tolerance to malaria to the prophylactic which had been praised for its efficiency on the Niger River in 1854. They proudly quoted in their despatch the following figures for sickness on the expedition. No case of sickness occurred in the lower part of the delta amongst 10 officers, 37 seamen and 12 Kroomen. Anyone who developed fever was cured by the Livingstone regime and his convalescence was rapid. They concluded that the fever was only formidable when allowed to go on unchecked.[7]

Livingstone discovered that he could not go beyond Tete because of the Cabora Bassa Cataracts. But he still did not give up his search for a healthy station. He ascended the Shire River thereby discovering the Shire Highlands in April, 1859. He was delighted with his find; almost by chance he had stumbled upon this elevated, healthy fertile land, about 3 500 feet above sea level. Both he and Kirk moved freely there without contracting fever. They came to the conclusion that there were two strains of malaria. First there was the milder form existing in the high plateau in contrast to the deadly, severe form in the mangrove swamps of the Zambesi. Whichever type became established had a tendency to recur. On their return to the *Ma-Robert*, they found Walton, one of the crew, severely ill with malaria. This puzzled Livingstone as Walton had taken his preventive quinine regularly. He decided that Walton had not taken sufficient exercise while he and Kirk were on shore and on this inadequate evidence abandoned the prophylactic quinine temporarily. When fever broke out severely in 1861 among the crew on the *Pioneer*, as it ploughed its way through the Elephant Marshes of the Shire, Livingstone reinstituted its use.[8]

Despite Livingstone's frequent writings in medical journals, the missionaries were slow to accept his advice. At times they even neglected it. This could be said of the Helmore Price Expedition, for, as soon as the missionaries and their families settled at Linyanti, described by Livingstone as a most unhealthy spot, they became ill with malaria. So bad were they that in the course of eleven months, six out of nine Europeans died of the acute form of the disease. The mission was abandoned and the Rev. Price and the two other survivors escaped from there. When Livingstone and Kirk reached Linyanti in 1860 and learnt of the disastrous start of this mission, Livingstone was greatly distressed. He was surprised that no attempt had been made by the members of the mission to treat the fever according to his earlier writings. So upset was he that he sent a special despatch to Lord John Russell, again giving details of his regime for malaria. It seems surspiring that, knowing how deadly was the fever in these regions, the first missionaries failed to take precautions to protect themselves after choosing to work in such an unhealthy part.[9]

Despite Livingstone's advice about the treatment of malaria, when the U.M.C.A. mission was coming out to the Shire Highlands, it had as tragic an end as the Helmore. The Mission did appoint a doctor, John Dickinson, and started on the site at Magomero chosen by Livingstone as a healthy one. But the doctor arrived late and by the time he came the mission was already beginning to crumble. Bishop McKenzie, its leader, being a layman, did not take the fever as seriously as he might have and when Dickinson arrived it had already started to take its toll. In addition, dysentery was rife and food stores somewhat depleted because of the many local inhabitants taken onto the station after releasing them from slave traders. It seems to have escaped the attention of the mission that only by complete regular dosage of quinine could the hazards of the fever be reduced although there would still be some degree of suffering. Whatever can be said about the failure of the first U.M.C.A. Mission, it should be remembered that it was the fever that drove the missionaries from the Shire Highlands. On Livingstone's Zambesi Expedition his men were exposed to it in its worst form in the marshlands of the low lying Zambesi. He and his party lived in these dreadful parts for nearly four years, plying up and down the rivers, yet, because of his strict regime for the management of the fever, the expedition survived instead of undergoing a similar fate to that of the Great Niger Expedition. The number of deaths was small in comparison with those of the U.M.C.A. mission that settled first at Magomero in the Shire Highlands and later on the shore of the Shire river itself. Another earlier, much smaller expedition, had ascended the lower Zambesi in a canoe in 1821. All three naval per-

28

sonnel on this expedition were carried off by fever in a matter of weeks. No mention of quinine was made.[10]

Comparing Livingstone's expedition with that of Tuckey up the Congo in 1816 and the later ascent of the Niger (1841–2), we realise what a tremendous difference the Livingstone regime made in the control and management of the fever. Only four Europeans died from May, 1858, to 30 June, 1863, in a period of five years of continuous exposure to a most severe form of malaria. Had it not been for David Livingstone's training as a medical man and his malarial regime he could not have survived the crossing of Africa. Even if a miracle had happened and he did live through this ordeal to lead his expedition up the Zambesi and discover Nyasaland, this would have ended in disaster.

NOTES AND REFERENCES

1. Gelfand, M. (1957) *Livingstone the Doctor. His Life and Travels.* Letter to Robert Moffat, Chonuane. 21 March, 1846. p. 39.

2. McWilliam, J. O. (1843) *Medical History of the Expedition to the Niger during the years 1841-2.* Comprising an account of the Fever which led to its abrupt termination. London, Churchill. Also see Wallis, J. P. R. (1956) Ed. *The Zambesi Expedition of David Livingstone 1858–1863.* Chatto & Windus. See letter David Livingstone to the Right Hon. Lord John Russell, 6 September, 1860. p. 387. Enclosure 1 in Despatch 9.

3. Schapera, I. (1960) (Ed) *Livingstone's Private Journals 1851–1853.* Chatto & Windus p. 47.

4. Livingstone, D. (1857) *Missionary Travels and Researches in South Africa.* Murray. London. p. 194.

5. J. P. R. Wallis (1956) Ed. *The Zambesi Expedition of David Livingstone (1858-1863)* Chatto & Windus, London. p. 351.

6. Gelfand, M. (1964) *Rivers of Death in Africa.* Oxford University Press, p. 62.

7. Wallis, J. P. R. (1956) Ed. *The Zambesi Expedition of David Livingstone 1858-1863.* See Enclosure No. 1. Reports on the African Fever to Sir James Clark. Remarks on the African Fever in the Lower Zambesi by David Livingstone and John Kirk. River Rovuma 25 March, 1859, p. 309.

8. Gelfand, M. (1957). *Livingstone the Doctor. His Life and Travels,* p. 223.

9. Wallis, J. P. R. (1956) Ed. *The Zambesi Expedition of David Livingstone, 1858–1863.* David Livingstone to the Right Hon. Lord John Russell, 6 September, 1860. Chatto & Windus. p. 393.

10. Gelfand, M. (1956) *C.Afr. J. Med.* 2. 403.

Livingstone the Geographer and Explorer*

UNVEILING OF THE LIVINGSTONE STATUE

The bronze statue of David Livingstone, placed on the north side of the Society's Hall, was unveiled by the Secretary of State for the Colonies (Mr Oliver Lyttelton) on Friday, 23 October, 1953. Prior to the unveiling ceremony the Secretary of State was received by the President of the Society (Mr J. M. Wordie), Dr Hindle, Dr Briault, General Sir James Marshall Cornwall, Mr Leonard Brooks, Mr T. B. Huxley-Jones and the Director and Secretary (Mr L. P. Kirwan).

The party proceeded to the Hall, the President took the chair, and with him on the platform were the Secretary of State for the Colonies, Dr Hubert Wilson, the General Secretary of the London Missionary Society (The Rev Maxwell O. Janes) and Mr T. B. Huxley-Jones.

The President, in opening the proceedings, said:

I should like this afternoon, by way of introduction, to speak about Livingstone's connection with our Society, and more particularly of his association and friendship with our great President, Sir Roderick Murchison.

Livingstone landed in Africa for the first time in 1840 and during the next ten years of what may be called his purely missionary period he undertook numerous journeys, many of them of more than 600 miles. On one of these, in 1842,

---

*Extracted from the Royal Geographical Journal, Vol. CXX, part 1. March, 1954 (pp. 15–20) by kind permission of the R.G.S.

travelling northwards he was within ten days' distance of Lake Ngami. Although he knew the lake was nearby he did not turn aside.

His first actual journey of discovery did not take place till 1849, when with Oswell and Murray he crossed the difficult Kalahari Desert and reached Lake Ngami itself, known only at that time by report. Although not widely recognised by the world at large, Livingstone's name soon came to the knowledge of the Society for Captain Steel, who had been associated with Livingstone during hunting expeditions, was a Fellow. Steel wrote to Sir Roderick Murchison and in this way there originated the long-standing association of the two men. Murchison at once realized the value of Livingstone's journey to Lake Ngami and the Society in turn showed its appreciation by the award of a chronometer watch to "The Reverend David Livingstone for his successful explorations in South Africa".

The missionary journeys were developing into explorations and Livingstone was now making himself expert in survey. He was searching for watered lands and the search culminated in his reaching the Upper Zambesi in 1851. At that time Livingstone had had a vision of possible waterways, both eastwards and westwards, which would allow of easy travel and commercial enterprise north of the Kalahari.

After a short visit to Cape Town so that his family could return to Britain, he himself went back to the mission station, and late in 1853 set out on the journey which was to take him from Linyanti on the Upper Zambesi to Loanda on the west coast, a difficult journey which showed that he was a very determined traveller. The return from Loanda began in 1855, but from Linyanti he travelled on eastwards down the Zambesi, discovered the Victoria Falls, and finally reached the east coast at Quilimane in the summer of 1856. This great journey across Africa from west to east made Livingstone famous, and the Society, which had already recognized his promise in 1850, now awarded him in 1855, while the journey was still in progress, their Patron's Gold Medal. We can take pride in our early recognition of Livingstone's genius.

He came back to this country in the autumn of 1856 for the first time after seventeen years. In the interval he had become a national hero. Shortly after arrival he attended a meeting of our Society, when he was enthusiastically received, and Murchison spoke in unqualified terms of the value of his discoveries. This meeting was an event such as can only take place very occasionally, when the whole country is aroused—the return of Shackleton in 1909, of Scott's companions after his last expedition in 1912, and in our own day of the Everest party.

Livingstone felt it his duty to return to Africa as soon as possible and before leaving he was entertained by the Society at a great public dinner in the Freemasons' Tavern, with Murchison presiding. There followed the Zambesi expedition which lasted from 1858 till 1864 when Livingstone found that there was no easy navigation, as he had hoped, up the Zambesi from the east coast. He was however seeking also for livable lands and found them up the Shire River on the nearby Highlands. Lake Nyasa was discovered in 1859.

Livingstone was again fêted and entertained on his return to this country, and during his two years at home he attended many of our meetings.

He left for Africa for the third and last time in 1866, following proposals by Murchison that he should explore the watersheds of the Nile, Congo and Zambesi. As on his first journey across Africa, Livingstone travelled alone with no companions other than native followers. Murchison was President for the fourth time and was anxious to remain in office till Livingstone should again come home. He would have retired earlier but stayed on in the hope that he might receive Livingstone on his return. This was not to be, and Murchison's last meeting as President was in November, 1870. He retired the following year and died a few months later. When the news reached Livingstone of Murchison's death he was deeply touched and wrote "Alas! This is the only time in my life I ever felt inclined to use the word, and it bespeaks a sore breast. The best friend I ever had—true, warm and abiding. He loved me more than I deserved."

The affection of these two men, great in their different ways, has been frequently remarked on. Some of it has been ascribed to their having both been of Celtic origin. I think this is almost certainly the case, and it should be noted that both had had ancestors who had suffered in the '45 Rebellion. The Murchison Monument on the shores of Lochalsh not far from Skye does not commemorate Sir Roderick, but was erected by Murchison himself in memory of his forbear, Donald, who had shown his devotion to his master, Lord Seaforth, by collecting as factor the rents on the Seaforth estates and forwarding them each year while Seaforth himself was in exile. This tribute to his ancestor is an unexpected side to Murchison, generally regarded as austere and aloof. Livingstone's connection with the '45 is less certain, though it is reported that his great-grandfather fought at the battle of Culloden, and an ancestor is reputed to have shown active sympathy for James Stewart of the Glens, another factor loyal to his chief, but who paid for his loyalty with his life.

Livingstone was to stay on in Africa till the end. He preferred to remain although his doing so gave rise to much anxiety and to false rumours of being "lost". He died on 1 May, 1873. There followed the romantic and almost incredible journey on which his faithful servants carried his body down to the coast, when Chuma, Susi and others earned fame by a nine months' journey of 1 500 miles from Chitambo's village to Bagamoyo, opposite Zanzibar. When the body reached this country it was met at Southampton by the President and Council of the Society and brought to London to lie in state very fittingly at the Society's House in Savile Row, prior to burial at Westminster Abbey. Dr Mill, the historian of the Society, has described the scene and the nation-wide feeling which was aroused. The history of the Trust Fund, from which the cost of the statue has partly been defrayed, extends over a longish period but may be briefly told. After Livingstone's death his faithful servants, before setting out to carry the body down to the coast, buried the heart at Lake Bangweulu at the place where their master had died, his name cut deeply in the solid wood of the tree marking the grave. This is the tree which may now be seen in our Museum, for in due course it was reported to be in a decaying state, and the lower portion was therefore cut out so that the famous inscription should be preserved. It was brought to this country in 1898.

The tree was replaced by the erection of a more prominent monument, a 20-foot stone obelisk set up in 1903; the balance of the moneys raised for this memorial was placed in a Trust Fund to be used for its upkeep.

In 1948 however the obelisk was taken over by the Northern Rhodesia Commission for the Preservation of Natural and Historical Monuments, who also undertook responsibility for the upkeep. As there was no immediate use for the Trust Fund after 1948 the Council of the Society decided that the capital should most properly be used for the erection of a statue here in London. The fund provided the nucleus, but I should also mention a generous donation made by Lord Catto, who at the time was Honorary Treasurer, without whose help the scheme could not have been carried out.

The next step was the selection of a sculptor and in this we were fortunate to have the advice of Mr William King, President of the Royal Society of British Sculptors. The choice ultimately fell on Mr T. B. Huxley-Jones and I think you will agree that he has been most skilful in his work, has succeeded in showing Livingstone as we would like to see him, and that our present house is the most fitting site for one so warmly welcomed and encouraged by our Society for nearly twenty-five years.

Dr Hubert Wilson (representative of the Scottish National Memorial to Livingstone Trust, Blantyre) then said: Mr President, Ladies and Gentlemen—As the grandson of David Livingstone I fear I am a disappointment because my mother was only a schoolgirl when her father died and her recollections of him were limited to when she was seven years of age and when Livingstone was last in this country. When my mother came out to Africa forty years or more after her father died we got some of the chiefs and headmen together and they told us exactly what they remembered of Livingstone in his early days. If you sat with one of Livingstone's last journals before you, you could not have caught those men out, so exact were they in everything they said.

I have always tried when in Africa to meet those who remembered my grandfather. I met one old man, one among many who remembered his coming to that part of the country although he was only a wee small boy at the time. He said: "We were children at the time and we always remembered Livingstone as the man who came out of the Lake and lived under the water because his hair was so straight and not like ours at all. Whenever we saw him doing anything we watched with all our eyes, because we had never before seen a man like him and we never knew what he would do. One day we saw him going away by himself among the reeds on the shore of the lake, so we crept up and hid in the reeds to watch what he did. He took something in his hands and we thought he was going to return into the lake or perhaps worship his ancestors. But he worked with his hands all over his head and brought his brains out on top of it. We had never seen a man who could bring his brains out." Actually Livingstone was washing his head and the people had never before seen soap lather.

This year I met a very old man not far from Abercorn in Northern Rhodesia. When he was told that I was the son of Livingstone's youngest daughter he said: "Then he must be the grandson of the man who ate eggs." I asked what he meant by that and the man who was with me laughed and said: "You know in those days the people here never thought of using an egg as human food. When Livingstone was not well he asked the people one day to get him some eggs which he ate, and he was remembered ever after that as 'the man who ate eggs'."

When I was in Bechuanaland this year, I saw the house that Livingstone built, the only part left being the first two courses of stone, and I cannot but think that they were put there by Livingstone's own hands because he would himself have laid the foundation of his house although others might complete it. It was in a lovely spot—a spot to be remembered.

I am very appreciative of all that this learned Society did in those past days to back up and to help my grandfather. In fact, the Royal Geographical Society has been a name to conjure with in our house as long as I can remember, and it is nice to know that Livingstone's statue has a place in front of the house of a Society which has such a long tradition of usefulness behind it. Our own Memorial in Scotland at Blantyre is a Mecca to which thousands of people come each year; among them many young folk and children. It is good that they should visit the memorial because Livingstone's example is one that is well worth following.

The President: And now I ask the Rev Maxwell Janes to add a few words. He is General Secretary of the London Missionary Society which sent Livingstone out to Africa in his early days.

The Rev Maxwell O. Janes: Mr President, Ladies and Gentlemen—In the Board Room of the London Missionary Society in Westminster there hangs a portrait of David Livingstone in the place of honour, immediately behind the chair in which sits the Chairman of our Board; every Director of the Society on entering the room finds his eyes focused upon that portrait, for Livingstone was one of the most famous of all the missionaries of the Society.

The Directors of the London Missionary Society rejoice today, Mr President, that the statue of Dr Livingstone is being unveiled so that all who pass along the busy street can be reminded of a great explorer and discoverer, and even more a great missionary. Brought up as he was in a devout Christian home, and being of an adventurous, chivalrous and altruistic nature, it is not surprising that when he read in a letter from a Dutch missionary in China that there was a great need for medical missionaries in that land, he responded to the call. He began to prepare himself by hard work and study for the life of a medical missionary, and when he felt ready he made an offer of service to the London Missionary Society. If you look among the various exhibits in the exhibition here today you will find the letter in which he made this offer.

Towards the end of his training Livingstone heard an address by Dr Robert Moffat, who later became his father-in-law and who was one of the Society's missionaries in Africa. Dr Moffat described how often he had stood on a height above Kuruman in Bechuanaland and seen clearly in the north the smoke of a thousand villages where the Gospel had not been proclaimed. That vision must have impressed

38

Livingstone, for at the end of the address he approached Dr Moffat and enquired diffidently whether he thought he would do for Africa. Moffat's reply was: "Yes, if you are prepared to leave occupied ground and push to the north." That sentence was prophetic of Livingstone's missionary career in Africa.

After a period of apprenticeship at Kuruman, during which he mastered the language and learned the ways of Africa with characteristic thoroughness, Livingstone began to trek north. Wherever he went he preached, and slowly built up little congregations of Christians.

As he moved northwards he sought vainly for healthy sites for new mission stations, until at last he stumbled on the Zambesi and was shocked to the depths of his soul by his discovery of the slave trade.

I think I am right in saying that all Livingstone's future exploration, exploration in which this Society took so great an interest and had so honourable a share, had, as its underlying motive, the opening up of a way into Central Africa for Christianity and commerce—twin agents, as he saw them, for the redemption of Africa from paganism and slavery.

As a missionary Livingstone was keenly aware of the overwhelming importance of the conversion of individual men and women to the Christian faith and he strove to bring men to Christ. But he was also keenly aware of the need to redeem Africa from social evils—poverty, ignorance, tribal warfare and, above all, slavery; the diffusion of better principles and the development of legitimate trade were urgent priorities, the legitimate trade to cast out the illegitimate.

Livingstone regarded the end of the geographical feat of opening the way into Africa as the beginning of the missionary enterprise; and in order to be free to pursue his discoveries he resigned from the missionary staff of the London Missionary Society and accepted Consular service in East Africa. But to the end he was a Christian missionary, preaching whenever occasion offered, even when he was ill and close to the end of his life.

As I began by saying, in the Board Room of the London Missionary Society Livingstone's portrait has the place of honour, above the Chairman's chair. That chair was made in Africa, in the workshops at our station at Mbereshi, in Northern Rhodesia. It was made by Africans who no longer fear slavery, who have been trained in craftsmanship, and in self-respect, and who draw their inspiration and comfort from the same Lord as did David Livingstone. They have been educated in the things of the mind and the body, and are responsible members of the Christian Church. Out of gratitude for what the London Missionary Society has done for them they gave that chair to the Society some little while ago. Whenever I go into the Board Room and see the portrait of Livingstone and the chair, I feel that eloquent testimony is borne to the value and importance of the redemptive work which Livingstone did. So I am grateful that our Society and yours has the opportunity today of sharing in this auspicious occasion.

The Secretary of State for the Colonies then said: Mr President, Ladies and Gentlemen—I am sure you have enjoyed the speeches to which you have just listened and in particular that of David Livingstone's grandson, couched in the most appropriate language and pronounced with the excellence that always calls forth the respect and veneration of those born south of the Border.

Now, Sir, when we look back upon the nineteenth century with the perspective of another half-century of distance run, we see that it was an age of great men. Foremost among them we see the heroic virtues of their age epitomized in David Livingstone to whose immortal memory we meet today to do honour. It can be said that Livingstone unlocked the door of the African continent and opened a new page in its history. His remarkable journeys across Africa, undertaken on foot with only a few African attendants and in the face of unimaginable hardship, led the countries of Europe to open up this unknown continent and at the same time laid before the world all the horrors of the slave trade. All the aspects of Livingstone's life and work combine to form one great humanitarian purpose. By penetrating the almost limitless and then unknown land of Central Africa, he brought the Word of God to the African people: he opened the way to trade and to the civilizing influence which followed it: and he exposed and attacked two scourges which overshadowed the people of Africa—the slave trade and the relentless tribal wars, with all their terrible tragedies of human suffering.

All here know well the love that Livingstone inspired in the Africans and the devotion with which his African attendants carried his body through unknown hostile country to the coast, to lie at last with his nation's other heroes in Westminster Abbey. Today, eighty years after his death, the unknown lands through which Livingstone passed in the twenty years between 1853 and 1873—Bechuanaland, Mozambique, the Belgian Congo, Northern Rhodesia, Nyasaland and Tanganyika—are each moving forward towards nationhood, in the great awakening of the African continent. We who have inherited the task of of helping the African people in their forward march can only try in humility to follow the example of patience, tolerance, humanity and dedication that his life set us.

Before I unveil the statue to Livingstone's memory I can do no better than recall to your minds the words in which Lord Curzon enshrined David Livingstone's claim to lasting fame at the time of the Royal Geographical Society's celebration in

1913 of the centenary of Livingstone's birth: "As a missionary he was the sincere and zealous servant of God. As an explorer he was the indefatigable servant of science. As a denouncer of the slave trade he was the fiery servant of humanity."

Those present then proceeded to the pavement on the north side of the Society's Hall in Kensington Gore, and the Secretary of State for the Colonies unveiled the bronze statue of David Livingstone.

"As Men are Everywhere Else"[1]

PROF. MAX GLUCKMAN

David Livingstone's great crossing of Africa from near the Victoria Falls to the west coast, back to the Falls, and thence to the east coast, was largely financed by the chief of the Makololo tribe. And this is what Livingstone wrote of the Makololo people:

"I have found it difficult to come to a conclusion on their character. They sometimes perform actions remarkably good, and sometimes as strongly the opposite . . . After long observations, I came to the conclusion that they are just such a strange mixture of good and evil as men are everywhere else . . . there are frequent instances of genuine kindness and liberality, as well as actions of an opposite character . . . By a selection of cases of either kind, it would not be difficult to make these people appear as excessively good or uncommonly bad."

This theme, that the observer must carefully count and compare his facts, runs through all Livingstone's writings. Sir Richard Burton once said that African mothers lacked maternal feelings and would sell their children to slavers for a few beads: Livingstone commented that this view was based on a single incident; and that one might similarly argue that English mothers lacked maternal feelings because some foundlings were abandoned by their parents.

Livingstone brought to his observations of African life and society a balanced, open mind, plus the care with which he collected his geographical data. And it is these qualities which make everything he wrote on Africa a century ago so valuable as records for both historians and anthropologists. Yet the passages showing these qualities are often neglected, perhaps because they threaten the mystique which has gathered about Livingstone the missionary carrying the Gospel, Livingstone the liberator fighting the slave-trade, Livingstone the explorer making down the heart of darkest Africa, all in the midst of a savage and red-handed people. He was dauntless, a man of great courage, who faced every obstacle, from disease and hunger and fatigue to the threats of armed warriors and marauding bands. But his own writings show that he was only very rarely in danger from the weapons of Africans. On the contrary, more commonly he was dependent on the peaceful welcome and generous hospitality and help with which, throughout central Africa, they helped him on his arduous way.

Professor Jack Simmons, in a short, popular biography[2] of Livingstone, stresses several times the absence of prejudice from Livingstone's observations on Africans. And he concludes that "in the course of his career [Livingstone] did more than any single man to alter the whole European conception of Africa and Africans". But I do not think that even Simmons has pushed this argument far enough. For he uses here Livingstone's work largely to illustrate the man's character, and to praise it. Praise is indeed due; but we need also an assessment of the political and social situation of African society itself. I feel that there still remains too much of the attitude instanced by Sir Reginald Coupland's comment on the decision of Bishop Mackenzie to fight the Yao slavers in the Shire Valley: "All Englishmen in the country, in the

44

minds of the natives at least," Coupland wrote, "would be entangled in their savage politics." It is the adjective, "savage" that is so revealing. Bishop Mackenzie's decision may have been ill-advised: but politics involving steel and fire are not peculiar to Africa. They are not only the prerogative of "savages". Politics in Africa were not essentially different from politics in Europe; and it is here that the riches of Livingstone's data have not been fully used by colonial historians. Most notably, this appears in the failure to assess why the Makololo treated Livingstone so liberally, and provided men and means for his attempts to open up trade-routes for them to the coast. In some part this was due to his character: but, in addition, he was, at that time, the key figure in Makololo foreign policy.

In his first book, Livingstone described how he went on behalf of the Makololo chief to negotiate what we would call non-aggression pacts with the chiefs to the north and west of the kingdom—including the chief of the Barotse, whom the Makololo had driven out of their homeland. Thus the Makololo chief financed Livingstone as a peace-making ambassador, somewhat outside the ordinary political system, to obtain peace on certain frontiers. He wanted this peace because he hoped to concentrate all his forces on the south-east border to face the militant Matabele. Originally the Makololo had been driven out of Basutoland, far to the south. They had fought their way north to the central plateau of Northern Rhodesia, and had settled in comfort on the uplands. The Matabele attacked them and drove them out, so they went west to conquer Barotseland. They did not like the swampy, fever-ridden plains of this river region, and pined to return to the plateau. But the Makololo were terrified of the Matabele. When Livingstone was away on his journey to the west coast, for example, his father-in-law, Robert Moffat, who was at the Matabele capital, sent stores to him by a small party of Matabele warriors. The Makololo were afraid to cross the river to receive the goods, and eventually the Matabele carriers deposited these on the bank, shouted they had discharged their duty, and returned home. Only after many days did the Makololo collect the goods; but dared not bring them into the capital, lest they contained Matabele witchcraft. The goods were stored under a shelter on an island.

In this terror of the Matabele, the Makololo chief had seen a hope in Livingstone. Livingstone was son-in-law to Moffat, who was a favourite of the Matabele king. If Livingstone would settle with the Makololo as missionary, perhaps influence could be brought through his father-in-law to induce the Matabele king to allow the Makololo to return in peace to the uplands. Hence they sent for Livingstone, hence they welcomed him, hence they supported him and financed him loyally; always they kept urging him to become their missionary. They undoubtedly liked and respected him for himself, but it was as Moffat's son-in-law that they wanted him permanently among them. They were not interested at all in the other missionaries who came to settle among them; and these languished, some to death, in the Linyanti swamps. Livingstone held before them this constant promise of peace; and he never fulfilled it.

If my interpretation of Makololo dealings with Livingstone is correct—and it is based on Livingstone's own writings—then it suggests that no study of Livingstone's work is complete without an attempt to analyse the internal political situation of the different African regions through which he travelled. This is most important in Makolololand, where he was resident for a long time, and where he was so dependent on the people. I can speak of Makolololand, for I have worked there as an anthropologist: but it is possible that similar interpretations could be made in other regions. This is a general lesson. But it also means that we must examine again the developments of Livingstone's character.

The story of his disastrous incapacity for leading Europeans, as against his skill with Africans, has been told fully. But no biographer or historian has mentioned the way he let down the Makololo. After all the support they had given him, he returned to their country for only a month; and the chief, in Simmons' words, "displayed a pathetically intense desire for English settlement in the Batoka Highlands, offering to set aside a defined part of his country for the purpose". But, Simmons goes on, "for the present, Livingstone could do nothing but express thanks for the offer and promise to consider it further". He had "performed his duty to the Makololo": he had indeed, I would say, done his duty by bringing home those Makololo who had marched with him to the east coast. In the larger duty he had failed to bring them their desired peace and protection. I have said that he did not fulfil his promise to the Makololo: I am tempted to put it more strongly that he broke faith with them. And I think he knew it: perhaps throughout his second expedition this knowledge may have been acting on him to shut him off from his British companions.

THE SCOLDING CHIEFTAINESS

When we look at Livingstone's actions, with understanding of the African societies among whom he moved, with their own problems and complexities, the picture changes somewhat. For in most accounts of his explorations, the Africans appear too much as painted figures on a backdrop, savage, warlike, superstitious, slaving, but won over by Livingstone's personality. Livingstone is built up till he dwarfs thousands of Africans, who are dismissed as tyrannical chiefs, sufferers

47

from slavers, slavers themselves—or helpful headmen by the way. Unhappily, this mystique—I can only call it "a mystique"—spoils Professor Debenham's otherwise excellent book[3] on Livingstone the explorer. Livingstone here becomes a pilgrim, who finally moves through "swamps of destiny" into the "slough of despond". And thus Debenham takes the vividness away from Livingstone's own records in which the Africans emerge as characters in their own right, "just such a strange mixture of good and evil as men are everywhere else". For instance, Livingstone recorded a long conversation he had with a rain-doctor in Bechuanaland, who confounded Livingstone's accusations that God, not his medicine, made the rain, by retorting that God, and not Livingstone's medicines, recovered the sick;[4] and there is a charming passage where he and his men were scolded, like a lot of children, by a Lubale chieftainess into falling in with her wishes because they could no longer face her biting tongue.

Another striking, neglected trait is shown in his descriptions of how he observed medical etiquette in the heart of Africa. He would never treat a patient unless the African doctor called him into consultation, or unless this doctor had given up the case. In consultation, he never corrected the doctor in the presence of the patient, but only in private. Finally, when he and Kirk were asked to treat the dying Makololo chief, Livingstone only agreed when "the female physician already employed" assented, and on condition that "she remained . . . in the Chief's establishment, on full pay". It was part of his genius for understanding Africans.

I find this element of understanding lacking in Professor Debenham's book; but nevertheless I feel that it is the best book yet written on Livingstone. For it does illuminate Livingstone's work as an explorer and geographer, and this is the work which has never been questioned. As a student of

48

Makololo politics, I myself feel he let down the African people who helped him most. Again, though his work in general led to the ultimate putting down of the slave-trade, it has been said that the immediate effect of his journeys was twice to open up territory to slavers. Personally, I do not agree with this, but he certainly depended, during his last journeys, on slave-traders' charity. And in the end his missionary work was incidental. But he undoubtedly made known central Africa to the world, as no other explorer has done. And it was because he was fundamentally an explorer that he finally became obsessed with the desire to go on and on through Africa, making more and more discoveries. It was this obsession that led to his breach of faith with the Makololo, this that led him to associate with his hated slave-traders, and this that led him to his death of disease in the swamps of Lake Bangweolu.

INSIGHTS—AND MISTAKES

Professor Debenham brings out the strength of this obsession very well. He also describes more clearly than anyone else has done the worth of the discoveries, and assesses them against our present knowledge of Africa. Most striking, are Livingstone's insights. He produced a hypothesis relating the direction of the Trade Winds to the rotation of the earth. He understood the difficult hydrographical problems of the Upper Zambesi region, where rivers may flow in opposite directions at different seasons. He saw correctly that the central plateau of Africa was a large, flat depression, with very slight elevations within it, but surrounded by a rim of higher hills. So that at the monsoon rains the rivers flooded into the lower parts of the depression, and when full might flow backwards across very low watersheds. The rivers broke through the rim, in cascades and waterfalls. These are but examples of remarkable thinking, which stand out from the general achievement of covering the country at all, of mapping on his traverses, and by reports of Africans and Arab traders, and of reporting in detail on climate, soil, water-systems, flora, fauna, and people. Debenham also brings out Livingstone's mistakes. They were of three kinds. First, there were the almost inevitable mistakes of the cartographer travelling in unmapped country, through swamp and forest, relying on the reports of others, and often impeded by clouds from making star-readings. Secondly, mistakes were caused when his instruments were damaged, or went wrong. Professor Debenham discusses, thus, a series of longitudinal readings which Livingstone took on his last journey and which got his rough maps out of shape, and led him to wander vainly in the Bangweolu swamps to his death. And here accidents of fate perpetuated his errors. His first voyage on Lake Bangweolu was made in a stolen dugout: the thieving paddlers would not go beyond a certain point, for it led into the territory of those they had robbed. This halt prevented Livingstone later from recognising where he was, and thus correcting the erroneous results taken from his damaged chronometers.

It is the third set of errors which are most striking when we try to understand Livingstone's character. After he had returned to the central Zambesi from the west coast, he started to survey the Zambesi downstream to see if it was navigable as far as the gorges below the Victoria Falls. To travel in easier country, he made one big detour away from the river; and thus by chance failed to see the Kebrabasa rapids. One sight of these would have convinced him that they could not be passed as normally navigable, and the whole character of his second expedition might have changed. He made the assumption that there would be no difficult cataracts, but only small rapids, on this stretch of river. Yet, Debenham points out, Livingstone's own figures for heights above sea-level showed that the river had a considerable fall somewhere on this stretch of its course. One can only conclude that Livingstone was so determined that the Zambesi should be navigable, that he misconstrued his own evidence.

SEARCH FOR THE SOURCE OF THE NILE

He was already exhibiting an obsessional trait about geographical facts which was to develop later into a conviction that he would find, in the Lake Bangweolu region, the Nile's sources. For a time he thought that the Nile might rise from the northern end of Lake Tanganyika, though again known heights made that extremely unlikely. He abandoned that idea only when he travelled with Stanley to the northern end. Now he met two Swahili-Arab traders who told him, correctly, of a region where four rivers rise close together and run in different directions; and he became convinced that this was Herodotus's description of the sources of the Nile. Determinedly he pursued his search for this region of fountains, and only occasionally did he admit that he might be seeking for the sources of the Congo. Here, indeed, bad luck dogged him: when travelling by dugout up the west bank of Lake Tanganyika, he had just escaped finding the exit to the Congo.

Professor Debenham brings out how these obsessions haunted Livingstone and drove him on his later arduous journeys. He always rejected, in the end, the sensible course, in his determination that one more effort would make him the true discoverer of the Nile's origins. He became convinced that Sir John Kirk, at Zanzibar, was not supporting him. To press on, he became dependent on his bitter enemies, the slavers. At all costs, his journey of discovery must be pressed on. He pressed it on to important explorations. He pressed it on to his death.

The "mystique" about Livingstone has been built up, quite

unnecessarily, to make him a hero for Europe. Yet it is also striking that, in many parts, he is also a hero for Africans: since in the new states of central Africa there are few men who can be revered by several African tribes, let alone by whites and blacks, at once. The people of what was Makolololand remember him for what they call his *butu*, his sense of human kindness. Here, maybe, not only in his mapping of lakes, rivers, and mountains, and despite his weaknesses and obsessions, lies one of his greatest achievements—that he provided the material, as Professor Simmons says, "to alter the whole European conception of Africa and Africans". In his journeyings he also gave the Africans a view of the Europeans they could admire. Perhaps one day Livingstone's memorial will be that whites and blacks in Africa will see one another, as he saw the Makololo: "just such a strange mixture of good and evil—as men are everywhere else".

NOTES AND REFERENCES
1. This essay, written in 1955, could not be brought up to date with references to more recent writings on Livingstone, since I was having an operation to remove a slipped disc, when I was asked to agree to its being reprinted. I would not change the main argument. The most important later books in my opinion are I. Schapera's editing of *Livingstone's Family Letters 1841–48 and 1849–56* (1959), *Private Journals 1851–53* (1960), *Missionary Correspondence 1841–56* (1961), and *African Journal 1853–56* (1963); and Gelfand's *Livingstone as Doctor* (1957)—for details see general bibliography.
2. *Livingstone and Africa*, by Jack Simmons. English University Press.
3. *The Way to Ilala: David Livingstone's Pilgrimage*, by Frank Debenham. Longmans.
4. Schapera has compared Livingstone's published account from his *Missionary Travels and Researches in South Africa* (1857) with what Livingstone wrote in *Livingstone's Missionary Correspondence 1841–56* (edited by Schapera, 1961), where the conversation which in the book is presented as very connected, appears at various points scattered through various letters, at pp. 63–4, 102–3 and 120–1.

David Livingstone's monogram carved inside baobab tree at Shiramba, Mozambique.

David Livingstone, M.D.

The exterior view of baobab tree showing the narrow entrance to the hollow section of the tree in which Quentin Keynes found Livingstone's carved monogram.

Dr Livingstone's Monogram, I Presume?

QUENTIN KEYNES

I have recently proved that it is not only twentieth century tourists and lovelorn couples who cut their initials on trees in Africa. The great Dr Livingstone did it too—when no-one was looking—a full century ago.

After three months of searching and hoping for just such a romantic link with the renowned explorer, I have now found one in the Zambesi Valley, and it is still perfectly legible. I could hardly believe my eyes when I first spotted it hidden away in the dark interior of an enormous hollow baobab tree standing on the southern bank of the lower Zambesi, deep in Portuguese East Africa. It seemed too incredible that no-one had ever noticed it before.

And it demonstrated dramatically that even the serious-minded Doctor had been unable to resist the almost universal impulse to "doodle" on, or rather, in this case *in* a tree!

I think the main reason this mark of Livingstone's has remained unknown for a hundred years is that it is not a simple "D.L." It is, in fact, a carefully carved *monogram* of those initials not easily recognisable as being the entwined first letters of this famous man's name—*unless the onlooker has a special familiarity with his signature*. This I chanced to have.

Moreover, from its position and appearance I would guess that the explorer hadn't really intended that anyone should

53

ever come across his historic "doodle" in later years. There is nothing at all remarkable in the area surrounding the tree that Livingstone could have wanted to commemorate—only the hollow baobab itself.

How then did it fall to me to be the person to discover this needle-in-a-haystack only a few weeks short of a century from the day the Doctor had secreted it there?

The story really begins in 1957. I was in New York at the time and received an auctioneer's printed list of some rare books and authographed letters that were to be sold shortly in London. In browsing through it my eye fell on the listing "Livingstone, David". There followed the description of a fascinating four-page letter dated "25 May 1859" entirely in the explorer's handwriting which included the remark that he would "deposit" the document "in a bottle ten feet Magnetic North from a mark + cut on the beacon . . ."

Romantic that I am, I had always longed to own an original manuscript written by Livingstone during one of his expeditions in Africa, and here was one about to be auctioned which seemed very unusual: the good man had actually buried it in a bottle at the mouth of the Zambesi in hopes that some passing ship might pick it up.

From my reading of boys' adventure books, I had always understood that explorers were in the habit of leaving their letters in bottles, but now I had a chance to prove this was so by acquiring this letter and flaunting it in front of my sceptical and unromantic friends!

A cabled bid to London got the letter for me against stiff and expensive competition—fellow romantics, no doubt. Subsequently, by dint of some sleuthing I found out that the priceless document had been consigned for sale by a descendant of Rear Admiral Sir James Donnet, a mid-19th century ship's surgeon. He must have been on board a patrolling

Royal Navy vessel that had put in at the delta of the Zambesi when Livingstone's bottled message was unearthed by a member of the crew.

After I had scraped together funds to pay for it, I unfolded it lovingly, had it photostatted, and read it over and over again. It was a sort of to-whom-it-may-concern message, addressed vaguely: "To — Commander of Her Majesty's Ship ——." In it Livingstone describes his trip up the Zambesi and Shire Rivers and tells in detail of his discovery of Lake Shirwa (Nyasaland). He asks that "salt provisions" be left at the Zambesi mouth for the crew of his paddle-steamer and adds: "Several members of the expedition have suffered from fever, but not in its severest form . . ." Then he signs it: "I am etc., David Livingstone."

I particularly noted the oddly looped "D" and "L" of his signature.

There was no question but that the ownership of this unique letter somehow "got" me. I soon decided that I must go to Africa and very roughly retrace the explorer's epic six-year paddle and trek in the Zambesi Valley area. It had taken him from 1858 until 1864 to complete, and resulted in his fully documented book *The Zambesi and its Tributaries* which was published in 1865.

It was the second great exploratory trip of his life. During the first he had crossed the African continent from the west coast to the east, had seen the Zambesi for the first time, and hoped that this mighty river would later prove to be an easy highway into the then unknown territories of central Africa.

A special flat-bottomed paddle-steamer was built for him to negotiate the river. It was one of the world's first "pre-fabs" and was put together after his expedition arrived at the mouth of the Zambesi.

But a twenty-mile stretch of inaccessible rapids called the

Kebrabassa thwarted his plans of paddling right up the river and led him to explore the Shire and other tributaries to the north of the Zambesi. It was this sidetracking which led him to the discovery of Lake Shirwa.

Two friends became so interested in my idea that they decided to come along with me: Tarquin Olivier, a third-year undergraduate at Oxford and son of Sir Laurence, and David Coughlin, an American first-year college student. Together we invested in a Land Rover station wagon in England and drove up to Livingstone's birthplace at Blantyre, Scotland— to begin at the beginning, so to speak. There is a museum now in the house where the explorer was born, and the trustees, greatly intrigued by our venture, gave us a letter for the Mayor of Blantyre, Nyasaland.

We took ship for Cape Town and soon were heading north to Rhodesia—a photostat of my bottle letter in my pocket at all times. Everywhere we went I would ask to be shown places that Livingstone was known to have visited. Whenever some gnarled old tree was pointed out that was said to have traditional associations with Dr Livingstone I searched its bark carefully for a possible "D.L."

An invitation came to us from a remote mission station at Lubwa, Northern Rhodesia. It was from Dr David Livingstone Wilson, a great-grandson of the explorer. I was astonished at Dr Wilson's similarity in looks to portraits of his forbear at a comparable age.

Did he know of any tree carvings? Only the well-known "D.L. 1855" that his great-grandfather had inscribed on a tree at the Victoria Falls shortly after discovering them, he said.

We bumped our way along a seemingly endless track towards the Congo border, to see the spot where Livingstone died in 1873. It was a grim place in nondescript bush country

56

—an obelisk with an inscribed plaque marks it today—and I couldn't help being moved by the thought that the explorer died there alone (except for his faithful African followers).

Later, although Livingstone never found it, we made a lengthy detour, via the Copper Belt and hundreds more miles of nondescript bush, to inspect the actual source of the Zambesi. A freshly-painted signpost announced this round pool of black water, which is fed by a spring in dark, moist forest near Kalene Hill, in the extreme north-western corner of Northern Rhodesia. A tiny beginning for a river that flows from here for more than 2 200 miles to its outlet in the Indian Ocean!

We crossed an unfrequented international border shortly thereafter, into Angola, and followed the Zambesi along the loop it makes into this Portuguese territory for nearly 200 miles.

We re-entered Northern Rhodesia near Balovale. The Zambesi here presented an impressive appearance as it meandered southwards along a tree-clad valley, but we left it temporarily to traverse the Kafue National Park.

At Katima Molilo, in the Caprivi Strip, we inspected an odd baobab tree. It boasted a small door at its base. Curious to see what was inside, I opened the door to find a spotlessly clean lavatory with cemented floor staring me in the face. "The former D.C.'s idea," I was told casually, as if a toilet-bearing baobab were a common occurrence.

At Mwandi (the old Sesheke)—furthest point on the Zambesi reached by Livingstone on his second journey—we were shown an ancient wild fig tree under which the Doctor was wont to preach to the inhabitants. Alas, I could find no initials on it. But when we came to the Victoria Falls I examined a baobab which was literally criss-crossed with people's initials —a glaring example of what the modern tourist will do if not checked.

I reflected sadly that the intials of the one man to whom no-one would begrudge such a display were now no longer visible at the Victoria Falls—although the Southern Rhodesian Public Relations Department, in a pamphlet I noticed at the railway station, hopefully announces that Livingstone's initials can still be seen on a tree at Garden Island, and even adds that these non-existent marks are 14 inches high!

When we drove our Land Rover across the bridge spanning the Zambesi here I was reminded that I myself could claim a connection with the river at this point: my own grandfather, Sir George Darwin, had opened this bridge officially in 1905.

At Chikwawa, Nyasaland, to which we made a detour, we had better luck over personal connections with the explorer. Two old chiefs, Kasisi and Masea, claimed that their fathers had been two of the 15 Makololo that the explorer was known to have brought with him to Nyasaland. Masea added an illuminating footnote: "The white man was very angry with my father because he had killed a buck on a Sunday. He said this was so bad that he was going to leave him an an illuminating footnote: 'The White man had proved to be stronger than the other Natives around Chikwawa, and had soon created themselves chiefs'."

We entered Portuguese East Africa and headed south to see what connections we could find with Livingstone in the last stretch of the Zambesi which flows through Portuguese territory to the sea. The main difficulty was going to be to reach the same Kebrabassa rapids which had ruined the explorer's plans of paddling all the way up river to the Victoria Falls. I asked several Portuguese officials if we could reach this rather inaccessible area by Land Rover. They shook their heads emphatically: "Only on foot," was always the reply.

Our schedule did not allow time for foot slogging. Yet I was determined to try to reach the rapids by bashing our way through in the faithful four-wheel-drive car. One Portuguese engineer, however, gave me hope: the year before, while on a survey trip to see about building a "Portuguese Kariba" at this section of the Zambesi, he had managed to get within an hour's hike of the river by jeep. Of course, he warned, a way had been prepared for him by labourers well in advance and no-one had been back along the scarcely discernible track since the rains early in the year.

But this merely made the trip more appetising to me. The "bundu" called, and we were off. It was only 13 miles, but it took us the whole of the first afternoon and most of the next day to get there and back. We had to crash through grass taller than the top of the vehicle, build up dried river beds with stones in order to cross them, and finally lay down a whole bridge of poles across a sizeable swamp before it could be negotiated.

On arrival at the rapids, which are strikingly situated between wild, tree-covered hills, we were so hot and exhausted that we plunged without a moment's hesitation into the swirling, muddy water of the Zambesi, and enjoyed a refreshing swim—crocodiles or no!

The country between Tete and the mouths of the Zambesi produced for us a sad association with Livingstone. At a small Portuguese mission station called Shupanga we found a walled cemetery. In a place of honour there a large, well-kept tomb with a brown head-stone at once attracted the eye. On it I could easily make out the following simple inscription: *Here repose the mortal remains of Mary Moffat, the beloved wife of Doctor Livingstone . . . she died in Shupanga House 27 April, 1862, aged 41 years.*

Our remaining objective now was the spot where the explorer had deposited my bottle-letter. But it was going to be difficult to find, partly because the true mouths of the Zambesi are remote from any settlements and partly because the Portuguese use different names from those appearing on the explorer's maps.

However, the British manager of a large Anglo-Portuguese sugar estate at Marromeau—the last place inhabited by Europeans before the Zambesi delta is reached—offered to help. The estate owns several paddle-steamers (sternwheelers) which are somewhat sturdier than the leaky old *Ma-Robert*, Livingstone's sidewheeler, which collapsed and sank midway through his expedition. It was near Chemba, in December, 1860, that the boat foundered. We searched unsuccessfully for its remains.

Our vehicle was lashed to a barge attached to one of the estate's quaint river boats, and, comfortably installed in mosquito-proof cabins on the top deck, we wheeled down to Chinde—a northern mouth of the Zambesi unknown in Livingstone's day—during the night.

There I at once sought out the local Port Captain. Could he help me identify the island at one of the true mouths of the Zambesi where Livingstone's party had erected a beacon a century ago?

He remembered once seeing a very old map in his office which at first he couldn't lay his hands on. Later an excited message came from him that he had found it. I hurried back and to my delight he gingerly unfolded a worm-eaten chart headed: "Mouths of River Zambesi, Surveyed by F. Skead, Master R.N., 1858-1861." There, plain as day, marked on an island called Inhamissengo within the "line of breakers" on the coast, I saw a symbol and the words "Signal Point Flagstaff". This was it. We must see if it still existed.

The Land Rover was off-loaded and we drove south-east, back to the main river. Taking about a dozen Africans, we then boarded two small motor-boats and chugged slowly down river. Immensely thick mangrove forests closed in on us from both sides, until we reached Inhangurue island at the mouth. Here we camped. Next morning we assembled the oldest inhabitants and asked them all the same question: Was there a tall pole on Inhamissengo across the waters, or did they ever remember seeing one in times gone by? Or had their fathers ever spoken of such a landmark? The answer was negative on all sides.

There were quite big waves in the three-mile stretch of light brown water which separated Inhangurue from Inhamissengo islands, but I decided we must risk a trip over to the latter in one of our small boats. I wanted to make certain Livingstone's beacon was no longer in existence.

We had seen an aerial photograph of the whole Zambesi delta in the Port Captain's office and from it we guessed that Inhamissengo island had been eaten away during the past hundred years by the relentless effect of the Zambesi's water rushing out to meet the sea. This was now confirmed from our boat. The explorer's "Signal Point" marked on the old chart was now a thing of the past—the coast line of this low island was utterly changed.

My disappointment over this was soon tempered, however, by what happened next.

In his book on the Zambesi the Doctor makes several mentions of a Portuguese named Senhor Ferrao whom he said had been of great assistance to him. On reaching a White Father's mission at Murraca I asked if there was still anyone in the area bearing that name. Yes, said one of the bearded Fathers, he did recall an old half-caste named Manuel Ferrao living some distance away, in the bush.

After some difficulty, we found a decrepit shack amongst banana trees, and the shy but intelligent Senhor Ferrao. I asked him if he had ever heard tell of a "Britannico" named

Livingstone. I will never forget the bright-eyed, almost lyrical expression his face assumed as he said: "You mean Dr David Livingstone? Why, certainly, Senhor. My grandfather knew him well and showed him where there was gold in the hills near Sena. And my father told me that when he was a young boy he remembered that the Doctor had given him a model boat to play with. My father said he was a tall man, and very kind." After some deep thought he added: "Have you not seen the hollow baobab tree near here where the 'Britannico' camped?"

I at once was reminded that a Portuguese government officer at Tete had mentioned a similar tree. He was not sure exactly where it was, but he was certain that this peculiarly formed baobab was a kilometer or two above or below a point where two tracks met near Shiramba. Now that two people had described this tree, it sounded well worth investigating, although I confess I was a bit sceptical, having already examined more than a dozen trees supposed to have associations with Livingstone—indistinct initials were frequently mentioned as well—only to have remained unconvinced every time.

But with this one I hit the jackpot. For this was the haystack in which I found the needle. And it appears to be the last remaining mark left on the trees of Africa which can be definitely attributed to Livingstone.

It was about three miles above Shiramba and an immensely wide baobab, easily distinguishable from others along the way by a narrow slit in its trunk. The slit provided a doorway taller than a man, and all three of us were able to walk upright through it into the tree's dark interior. Here we found a perfect natural shelter which I estimated to be over 30 feet high and perhaps 30 feet around.

Excitedly I peered around for initials. There were several newly-made ones and some indistinct—rather older—marks.

But nothing that looked remotely like "D.L." Then I turned to face the entranceway—and there, a foot or so from the edge of the slit, was the mark which I immediately deciphered as the work of David Livingstone from the characteristically looped "D" and "L" of his signature that I had long since noted on my bottle letter. I could see it had been cut a long time ago from the blackness of the indentations.

"Dr Livingstone's monogram, I presume?" I said to my astounded companions.

In camp that night, I searched through a printed copy of the explorer's Zambesi diaries and found an entry which clearly and indisputably confirmed my discovery. Under date of September 16th, 1858—it was now August, 1958—I read: "We wooded at Shiramba, about four miles above the spot pointed out as the great house . . . I walked a little way to the south-west and found a baobab which Mr Rae and I, measuring about three feet from the ground, found to be 72 feet in circumference. It was hollow and had a good wide high doorway to it. The space inside was 9 feet in diameter and about 25 feet high. A lot of bats clustered about the top of the roof and I noticed for the first time that this tree has a bark inside as well as out."

It seems evident from the last sentence that Livingstone had been playing around with his penknife on the inner surface of this strange hollow tree, and that he had, probably without thinking much about it, soon manufactured this perfect monogram.

The experts seem to agree with me. Dr Hubert Wilson, the explorer's grandson—to whom I showed my flashlight photograph of the monogram when I visited him in Scotland at the end of my Zambesi trip—unexpectedly found that he had the particular original manuscript diary in his possession containing the pages with the above entry.

Professor Frank Debenham of Cambridge University, generally considered to be one of the greatest living Livingstonian scholars, said to me that he thought the monogram was undoubtedly cut by the Doctor.

"If he'd carved it on the live, outside bark of this baobab it would have grown over in a very short time," he continued. "This is what happened to his celebrated 'D.L.' at the Victoria Falls. But because the tree's hollow inner surface was already dead in 1858 there would have been no change in it since. That's why the monogram was still there for you to discover in 1958!"

The Mozambique Government has since declared the Shiramba baobab an historical monument in honour of David Livingstone.

"Livingstone's Criteria of Advancement with Reference to the Malawi of Today"

PROF. BRIDGLAL PACHAI

In a centennial stock-taking exercise of Livingstone's impact on Malawi it would be useful to recall three common features: his general guidelines of Christianity, commerce and civilization; his bringing out of the Kololo immigrants to Malawi in 1860, who remained in the country after his departure in 1864 as leaders in the lower Shire area, afterwards setting the pace in supporting schools and missions run on western lines; his indirect and direct contribution towards the proclamation of British protectorate rule in Malawi in 1891 at the expense of Portuguese imperialism which he had stirred into action and which he left to his successors in both religion and politics to frustrate and put out of commission. All these three general features carry Livingstone's clear imprint. But of far greater importance are the particular features of agriculture, commerce, education and evangelisation in which Malawi had for long led the way in Central Africa in the post-Livingstone era.

This is not to say that the implementation of either the general or the particular features was based wholly on the Livingstone concept or plan. Indeed there were important departures and variations though it would be difficult to deny

65

that the impetus which marked the beginnings and early stages of the realization of most of them could be traced to Livingstone or to the period and programme which he symbolized.

AGRICULTURE

Livingstone held the view that Malawi was good cotton country all the way from the Shire-Zambesi confluence to the lake and that some cotton was being grown in every village. The first cotton gins were brought to Malawi by Livingstone's Zambesi Expedition in 1858 and a beginning was made to purchase cotton from the African villagers so that they would appreciate the commercial possibilities of their own genuine industry as contrasted with the living made by slave raiding and trading. It was believed in some circles that the Malawi-grown cotton was superior to the American brand and capable of realizing a profit of 400 per cent on the British market. There were, of course, doubts expressed at the time locally and abroad about Livingstone's expansive enthusiasm over cotton cultivation and prospects, especially by Reverends James Stewart and Henry Rowley and by certain overseas correspondents to *The Times*, London.

But later events, especially since 1903, proved Livingstone's optimism to be well-founded. In that year the British Cotton Growing Association was formed and Malawians were encouraged to take to cotton cultivation. In the first year (1904) they produced 26 tons of cotton; ten years later the figure rose six-fold. By then the cotton industry, both European and African, was the largest in the country, accounting for over 40 per cent of the exports, a clear vindication of the promise Livingstone saw in cotton production. Though cotton has in more recent times given way to tea and tobacco it still ranks among the big three. It is an important African industry with considerable promise for the future as the Chikwawa Cotton

Agricultural Project and the Salima Agricultural Project, two of the more ambitious cotton cultivation schemes in Malawi, continue to expand.

COMMERCE

Besides commenting on the agricultural potential in Malawi, Livingstone realized that British businessmen would profit in any venture in which raw materials could be obtained in Central Africa to boost British manufacturers. At the same time new markets would be opened up for British manufactured goods. Livingstone informed Sir Roderick Murchison the President of the Royal Geographical Society of these possibilities and left it to him "to give a few hints" to merchants and travellers. As a practical man, Livingstone no doubt realized that would-be supporters of missionary enterprise needed to be assured of financial returns.

The higher objective he had in mind was that the entry of legitimate commerce would help in the fight to drive out the illegitimate traffic in slaves. He alluded to this in his famous Cambridge address on 4 December, 1857: "The natives of Central Africa are very desirous of trading, but their only traffic is at present in slaves . . .: it is therefore most desirable to encourage the former principle, and thus open a way for the consumption of free productions, and the introduction of Christianity and commerce . . ."

Livingstone felt that missionaries could also be traders since the promotion of Christianity and commerce were complementary to each other. In Malawi this did not work out in quite that way though the earliest attempt was based on this possibility through the initiative of Rev. Dr James Stewart who came out to Malawi in 1876 at the head of the second party of Livingstonia missionaries. In that year he wrote to the Glasgow Livingstonia Committee asking for permission to open a store, arguing that "No sermons or daily lectures on the benefits of industry and the sin of idleness would accomplish one-twentieth part of the good that would be achieved by a single depot of goods here, where people could get what they want in return for what they have . . ." Stewart already had in his party one H. B. Cotterill, son of the Bishop of Edinburgh, with some £500 worth of trade goods. This one-man enterprise did not succeed while the Glasgow Livingstonia Committee expressed its disapproval of missionaries acting as traders. The business side was placed on a separate and formal basis when the Livingstonia Central Africa Company (afterwards known as African Lakes Company and finally African Lakes Corporation) was formed in June, 1878, with an anticipated capital of £20 000.

This company pioneered commercial enterprise in Malawi opening up the country for legitimate trade, often acting in various other roles as well. In later years it was joined by other trading concerns, none of which surpassed its field of operations. Its popular name "Mandala", though less noticeable in 1973 than some ninety years previously, has survived as a reminder of one of Livingstone's cherished pillars of advancement in Malawi.

EDUCATION AND EVANGELISATION

The leading propagators of mission work in Malawi in all its aspects, school, church, medical, agricultural, industrial and technical, both European and African, were connected directly or indirectly with the Livingstone heritage for Central Africa. This is to say that some of this work was begun during Livingstone's lifetime while the remainder started after his death; some, again, were closely linked to his own ideas while others were independent of them or departures from them.

It was Livingstone who was directly responsible for the

Obelisk and Plaque erected on the spot where Livingstone's heart is buried, at Chitambo's village, Zambia.

Emaciated slaves from a dhow captured by the British Navy in East African waters.

coming out of the first Mission to Malawi, the Universities' Mission to Central Africa, in 1861. He was partly responsible for the failure of this enterprise through his willingness to use force to suppress recalcitrant African communities and through his recommendation that the enterprise should begin operations at Magomero, a thoroughly unhealthy spot for the European members of the Mission as well as being too far from the points of southern entry into or northern exit from Malawi. Livingstone was extremely disappointed when Bishop Tozer decided to remove the Mission temporarily to Zanzibar from where a new start could be made, reinforced by African teachers and evangelists. It was with precisely this sort of reinforcement that the later U.M.C.A. stations succeeded in returning to Malawi in 1885 and extending its work of education and evangelization, being the first to ordain an African minister of religion, the Rev Johanna Barnaba Abdallah in 1898.

Livingstone, too, did not ignore the African side of the training and, like the later Scottish missionary, Rev. Dr David Clement Scott (Blantyre 1881–1898) often found it easier to work with Africans than with Europeans. Among the slaves whom Livingstone set free at Mbame's village on the outskirts of Blantyre a number went on to become devoted mission workers and afterwards entrepreneurs in their own right, persons like Tom Bokwito, Sam Sambane and Wakotani, all three of whom helped the later Livingstonia and Blantyre Missions in various ways. It is no wonder, then, that a village headman with the name of David Livingstone still resides in the locality of the former Mbambe village a hundred years after Livingstone's death.

The first two of them were sent to Lovedale Mission in South Africa in 1864, while the third was taken to Bombay by Livingstone himself later to return and help to instal the Livingstonia Mission at Cape Maclear in 1875.

More than that from the African side was the fact that fourteen Africans from Lovedale offered to come out to Malawi in 1876 to serve as teachers and evangelists. Four were chosen, William Ntusane Koyi, Shadrack Ngunana, Mapas Ntintili and Isaac Wauchope Williams. From the pen of Shadrack Ngunana we get this helpful description of life at Livingstonia as he saw it at Cape Maclear on 29 November, 1876: "Behind Livingstonia there are stony mountains towering up beautifully, shutting us out from the villages round about. But I am glad to say that natives come here nearly every day; some bringing articles for sale, such as potatoes, mealie-flour, raw cotton, native pots, fish, Kaffir corn, maize, fowls and goats. The selling of these things generally takes place in the evening, and we may say at present the market place is near the dining hall, where you could see Mr Johnstone or Mr Simpson spreading their blue cloth and measuring it into yards and fathoms. All these are brought as provisions for the mission. Others are coming for work. On some weekdays they are gathered in a hut before dinner, and a certain subject is explained to them. On Sabbaths they are taught the word of God."

This account would have pleased Livingstone because it bore out most of his own expectations to some extent: encouragement of African agriculture and trade; employment opportunities; the spreading of civilizing influences together with that of the message of God (the church and the school).

Both the Blantyre and the Livingstonia European missionaries did useful work towards the realization of the Livingstone expectation. That they did not succeed overnight in bringing about a Christian or economic revulution was not due to lack of industry or effort on their part; that they laid the foundations upon which future development would be based cannot equally be denied.

In the areas of education and evangelisation the products of the Scottish missions in particular, though by no means exclusively, paved the way for African development not only in Malawi but in various countries in east, central and southern Africa. Many of them left Malawi to assume positions as teachers, clerks, civil servants, capitaos and church leaders in these areas. Some of the more famous of these persons were Daniel Malekebu, Kamuzu Banda, Alexander and Isaac Katongo Muwamba, Clements Kadalie, Robert Sambo, Dinneck Kwanje, Ephraim Semu, Andrew Mbanda, Issa Macdonald Lawrence, Kamkati Mkandawire and Hanock Msokera Phiri. Others like John Gray Kufa, Rondau Kaferanjila, Harry Matecheta and Lewis Mataka Bandawe served as teachers and evangelists in outstations as far away as Mozambique. Few, like Clements Kadalie and Ephraim Semu, never returned to Malawi but most of the others did and in due course obtained positions of importance as businessmen, farmers, teachers, Church leaders and proto-nationalists.

They and their kind were the agencies of development and change in Malawi. Their old way of life was affected through various influences, both African and non-African and they were called upon to adjust and adapt. That they were, broadly-speaking, able to do so in such a short space of time must surely represent credit to themselves as well as to those European missionaries who acted as catalysts.

Because development in any country must touch the majority of the people it is in that group that impact must best be measured. The leaders, as everywhere, were few; the followers, as everywhere, were many. Some of the leaders were content to remain in the main stream of European enterprise and initiative. Their followers were those who conformed. There were other leaders who were wary of a permanent pattern of conformity where leadership was of external origins. As they matured in confidence and experience these "non-conformist" individuals gave expression to their own initiatives: John Chilembwe started the Providence Industrial Mission in Chiradzulu in 1900. This was carried forward from 1926 through to the year of the centenary of Livingstone's death by Dr Daniel Sharpe Malekebu, first American-trained Malawian medical-missionary. Then there was the formation of the African Methodist Episcopal Church by the Kasungu-born Rev. Hanock Msokera Phiri, in 1924, followed by the setting up of independent schools in the next few years. In northern Malawi, Kamkati Mkandawire started the African National Church in 1928 while between 1933 and 1934 two ex-ordained ministers of the Church of Central Africa Presbyterian, Yesaya Zerenji Mwase and Charles Chidongo Chinula started their own churches and schools. Mwase founded the Nyasaland Blackman's Educational Society while Chinula organised the Sazu Home Mission. One of their erstwhile supporters, Levi Zililo Mumba, surely one of the most outstanding mission products in Malawi in the early twentieth century, went on to become the first secretary of an African voluntary association, first African grade one clerk, first African member of the Advisory Committee on Education and first president of the Nyasaland African Congress. In one of his many fights for African advancement on the Advisory Committee he told his fellow European members: "Educate for the employer, educate for service with tribal communities, but most of all educate the masses to stand on their own feet. Give us this chance and I can assure you that within a period of a comparatively few years the response of the Nyasaland African will be surprisingly great."

If Mumba was the epitome of development in Malawi, he was also in a great way a Livingstone by-product in that he represented the fruition of an earlier dream that when Christianity, commerce and civilization found their foothold in Malawi many generations would benefit from their combined operation.

Livingstone and Education

DR NORMAN ATKINSON

If a man's greatness is judged in terms of his influence on successive generations after his own time, then Livingstone has had few equals in Africa. He was, in the first place, the most outstanding example of a new type of Christian missionary, whose work was concerned not only with saving souls, but also with an active participation in social reform. In the second place, he played a leading part in turning the attention of British imperial statesmen towards their responsibilities to African people committed to their care. Though Britain's social conscience had already been stirred by Wilberforce and the Anti-Slavery reformers, it was from Livingstone that British people learned for the first time of the immensity of the task which faced them in bringing African communities into contact with the mainstream of Western civilisation. Finally, and almost certainly most important in the long run, he taught African peoples to appreciate that an acceptance of Christian teaching and Western standards of life need not necessarily prove incompatible with the preservation of much of their own traditions and culture.

Livingstone's involvement with Africa was in large part determined by the influences of his own early life. He was a product of the democratic educational traditions of Scotland which, in contrast to those of England, provided encouragement for people of humble background to reach the highest levels of academic learning. This did not mean that he was "self-educated", except in the sense in which all men of learning are necessarily self-educated. The story which he himself told of how, having begun work in a Lanarkshire cotton-factory at the age of ten, he studied Ruddiman's *Rudiments of Latin* by placing it on the spinning jenny and reading as he passed to and from in the course of his work, has frequently been misunderstood. But it implied that the instruction which he received, first for many years at evening school, then afterwards in Glasgow University, had to be paid for through the sweat of his own brow. At the same time the broad-based approach of the Scottish curriculum allowed him to delve into many different branches of humanitarian study. Long before he turned his mind to theology he had a special interest in botany, geology, zoology and other scientific subjects, whilst as a medical student at Anderson College he insisted on attending Greek classes in winter and divinity classes in summer.

The effect of these influences was to leave Livingstone with an unusually well-developed sense of the role of education as an instrument of social and economic progress. Once having committed himself to Africa—after the outbreak of the opium war in 1840 frustrated his original intention of missionary work in China—he embarked on a vigorous programme of exploration intended to open up a deeper understanding of the continent and the life of its people. The impact on the outside world was certainly very considerable. A number of his more spectacular exploits—notably the discovery of Lake Ngami in 1849 and of the Victoria Falls in 1855—not only inspired renewed iterest in geographical and scientific exploration of the African interior, but encouraged the foundation of the Universities Mission to Central Africa in 1857. Only, perhaps, in the slowness of British Universities in introducing African studies as a regular part of the curriculum—the first university department specifically committed to African studies was organised at London during the 1930's—was there some indication of a lost opportunity.

Educational considerations were evident in Livingstone's development of a new missionary strategy, based on the production of a class of African teachers who might be expected to carry Christianity and other civilising influences among their own people. He was not unaware of the economic advantages of a system which would allow a much wider extension of missionary activity than could be possible through the labours of European colleagues alone. Yet he laid much greater stress on the special educational qualities of African teachers, "their warm affectionate manner of dealing with their fellow countrymen", and "their capability to bring the truth itself before their minds entirely divested of that peculiar strangeness which cleaves to foreigners". In Livingstone's view, it was only through a policy of self-reliance that African people could be led to achieve a lasting marriage between their own and Western culture. "I am more and more convinced," he said, "that in order to (effect) the permanent settlement of the gospel in any part, the natives must be taught to relinquish their reliance on Europe."

During the first decade or so of his stay in Africa he attempted to give a trial to the traditional missionary practice of organising schools with European teachers. The stations which he established for the London Missionary Society at Litubaruba, Mabotsa and Chonwane all had schools under his own meticulous supervision. "One of the most pleasant features," he wrote of Mabotsa, "is the progress made by the children in the infant school under Mrs Edwards . . . it shows what an amount of influence may be exerted over a country by the devotedness of a single individual. The parents form a mighty contrast with their fellow-countrymen still in darkness, and it is nearly as great between them and their children." And of Chonwane: "I began school and the foundation of our house on the same morning. The chief (Sechele) acquired a perfect knowledge of the large and small alphabets in two days and has since made considerable progress in learning to read. Fear of divorce in the event of his becoming a Christian makes his wives unwilling to follow his example, but he compels them to learn and is himself their teacher . . ."

These activities were brought to a summary conclusion by Livingstone's first and most impressionable contact with racial conflict in southern Africa. His use of African teachers aroused the animosity of the Afrikaner farmers of the Cushan Mountains, who had already trekked inland to escape British domination, and who feared that their position was now being threatened in a more insidious way. Livingstone was deeply affected by what he considered to be acts of unprovoked cruelty and injustice committed by the "Boers" on the defenceless local tribes. Yet even more significant was his realisation, perhaps alone among Europeans in southern Africa during his day, that unchallenged ascendancy by any one racial group carried in itself the seeds of eventual decay: "The emigrant Boers, who despise the law of benevolence enunciated in the declaration that 'God hath made of one blood all the nations of the Earth', are themselves becoming as degraded as the natives whom they despise. A slave population everywhere works the ruin and degradation of the free class which employs it."

No form of "rapprochement" with the Boers proved possible. Hendrick Potgieter, their leader, went out of his way to obstruct the work of the L.M.S. missionaries, and even went so far as to threaten with attack any African tribe which received a teacher. During 1852 he destroyed Livingstone's

77

home and possessions at Kolobeng. It was the heaviest psychological blow which the missionary had yet received in Africa. "I had a fine medical library," he wrote plaintively, "and many good works on general subjects. The former was my pride and a great comfort." Yet he was also led to take certain courageous decisions concerning the future scope of his operations: "I have got lightened, and will move so much more easily now." The intensity of Boer animosity had convinced Livingstone that his policy of working indirectly through African teachers was the right one, and should be carried out much more assiduously than before. Henceforward, he concentrated his efforts on opening up the land through exploration, leaving the foundation of permanent mission-stations to others.

This did not mean that he was altogether without memorial in the form of educational institutions established under his influence. Though the Portuguese slave-traders of the Zambezi region struck him as much more humane in their treatment of Africans, he was nevertheless concerned with the social and moral effects of their traffic on both slave and slaver alike. Whereas, on the one hand, the Portuguese appeared to be doing little or nothing to raise the tone of the indigenous peoples whom they ruled, on the other hand they were themselves in danger of decay through intimate contact with uncivilized people. The great problem, as Livingstone saw the situation, was how to remind Portuguese rulers of their duty to educate and elevate standards among all their people. The solution which he advocated lay in the establishment of large, well-established mission stations, capable of countering the influence of the slavers through the production of African experts in a wide variety of fields. One of the sites which he chose, near the shores of Lake Nyasa, was used after his death for the foundation of the Church of Scotland Livingstonia

Mission in 1875. And Livingstonia became the prototype of a number of similar institutions in Nyasaland, designed to provide African communities with clergymen, teachers, evangelists and technicians belonging to their own people.

Amongst all memorials to Livingstone, none is more significant than the name of the Munali Training Centre, established by the Northern Rhodesia Government in 1938 to provide a comprehensive range of facilities for African secondary education. "Munali", the name by which Livingstone was invariably known among African people, has remained unchanged in the days of an independent Zambia. The humanitarian values which Livingstone exemplified in his career have carried a lasting appeal to all the peoples of Africa, regardless of race, religion or political allegiance. In his memory there is hope for reconciliation and fellowship to come.

Livingstone's Campaign to Eradicate the African Slave Trade. A Brief Review of his Efforts and their Results

B. W. LLOYD

There has been a growing interest (particularly since 1945) in all phases of Africa's past. This Centenary in 1973 affords opportunities to review Livingstone's major part in a Campaign begun by Wilberforce and Clarkson, and reinforced by Buxton's great publication of 1839: "The African Slave-Trade and its Remedy" (reprinted 1967, Cass). Undoubtedly this work greatly influenced Livingstone's thinking in the years of preparatory exploration up to 1849, before his major African journeys led to his campaign to eradicate the evils he exposed in 1857 by his "Researches".

Livingstone first encountered the Arab slave trade in 1853 in Barotseland, but in 1859 saw in Nyasaland its worst results. On the Zambesi, 1858/64, he also saw the Portuguese trader active in destroying peaceful trade. Livingstone aimed at substituting "legitimate" trading, in place of the slave trade. Hence Kirk's aid to discover what crops could be grown, and Livingstone's attention to soils, minerals and African products likely to become exportable. From 1864/73 he did everything he could to attack the terrible results of the Arabs' grip on East Africa. In this he led public opinion in

England, conscience-stricken as it was since the days of Clarkson, Wilberforce and Buxton. Seven years after Buxton's death in 1845, Livingstone started his campaign to bring Christianity, Commerce and Civilisation into the heart of Africa.

In recognizing to the full such intrepid missionaries of the pioneer period, we must remember the chain of events. This was pointed out in 1931 by J. Huxley in his book "Africa View": "Without the Missionary spirit we should never have had Livingstone; without Livingstone the exploration and opening up of Africa would have been long delayed . . . The ghastly crime of the slave trade would have lasted many decades longer . . . In the unsettled conditions of those early days they played a vital role." (Page 319.) Nor must we overlook the fact that Livingstone's activities led to Stanley's exploits, which in turn produced the Congo.

In the light of experience, Livingstone restated his missionary policy before he renewed his efforts to open up a river route into Central Africa along the Zambesi in 1858. His Journal rejects the aim of simple conversion to Christianity in favour of plans to allow Missions to promote commerce. (This pleased the Glasgow and other merchants who backed his plans.) Commerce alone would destroy tribal isolation, and make tribes "mutually dependent on, and mutually beneficial to each other". Commerce, moreover, would enable "the Negro family" to be introduced into the body corporate of nations, and slavery would be destroyed. All this was according to the best Buxton plan.

These facts helped to form Livingstone's opinion that the usual picture of a Missionary going about solely with a Bible was incomplete. He, too, thought that efforts to promote trade widely would in the end be more beneficial than the work of individuals labouring with single tribes.

81

"Neither Civilisation nor Christianity can be promoted alone; in fact they are inseparable." In England, he appealed in his Cambridge and other lectures for help in the projects which eventually led to widespread missionary work. He strongly advocated free trade in Africa, and held that laws which hindered it even among civilized nations "seemed to be nothing else than the remains of our own heathenism".

From 1858, following his "First Missionary Travels and Researches" (1857) which the public avidly read, he had the active sympathy and support of the Governments of the day, of the Prime Minister, Palmerston, and of Clarendon, as Foreign Secretary. As "British Consul to the Interior of Central Africa", he was sent, with Portuguese approval, to be a "floating investigator" of conditions in the Zambesi valley and its tributaries. The failure of this expedition to find a river route to the Makololo country led to its diversion to Lake Nyasa, and its ultimate recall. But it did result in the formation of the Mission to Nyasaland, the founding of the Universities Mission to Central Africa and ultimately of the African Lakes Corporation (1878). These were all steps in ending slavery in the region which cut across the routes of the dhow slavers from Kota-Kota, their collecting centre. Livingstone's steamer on Lake Nyasa was the first blow to their system. His expedition to Lake Nyasa led eventually in 1891 to the Protectorate over the lake region being proclaimed by the British Foreign Office. This step was inevitable since early missionaries had found serious difficulties in acting as magistrates. Before the 1890s, there was no administration, no central government at all, and no transport faster than the pace of African porters.

Without the Foreign Office support and the watchful, continuous naval patrols round Zanzibar, where Kirk kept up his pressure on the Sultan's monopoly of slave selling, Livingstone's lone efforts far inland would have been unavailing. In fact, when he died in 1873, he was a disappointed man, not knowing of Kirk's treaty with Sultan Bargash, which closed the market in Zanzibar. The treaty was only concluded when the Sultan realised that, unless he yielded, the British Navy would blockade his island and close the market. After 1876, the Arab slave trade virtually ended when the Sultan decreed that in future no slaves could be transported through his dominions *by land*. This was a great victory for the Abolitionists, and for the belief, which first Buxton, and then Livingstone, had publicly championed for thirty years—that only on land could positive action to end slavery be successful. It also vindicated Livingstone's strong advocacy of British naval control of the African Coast as far northwards as possible, in order to prevent the constant smuggling out of slaves by Arba dhows.

Livingstone had no great belief in the persistent efforts to uproot the Slave Trade by diplomatic pressure on the Sultan of Zanzibar, the ruler of the infamous and lucrative market where about 20 000 survivors out of 250 000 slaves were sold annually. (Of these the British Navy only managed to free some thousand per year from 1815 to 1873.) A few of these are shown in an illustration below.

These figures do not detract from the persistent and determined efforts of Sir John Kirk to carry out the aims of Livingstone's campaign (see footnote). Another firmly held conviction was the great truth Livingstone constantly affirmed, that unless Africans produced sufficient cash crops (such as he endeavoured to introduce), there was always the danger of their reverting to the sale of their fellow-men. Without such products the Arabs had little difficulty in purchasing the victims of inter-tribal wars from such dominant chiefs as the Yao in Malawi.

83

The third principle of his faith was that which led him to Africa to spread the gospel of Christianity among her peoples. He continued to do so long after his leaving the L.M.S. in 1856. The accusation of his having "sunk the missionary in the explorer" is belied by his subsequent journeys (which may well be compared in "perils oft" to those which St. Paul endured over a period of approximately 17 years).

Livingstone's three great journeys, penetrating from East to Central Africa, through the great plateau of what is now Zambia, and into the lake region and highlands of present-day Tanzania, led him to advocate a chain of mission stations extending across the central sub-continent. Today, these mission stations, often equipped with hospitals, high schools and teacher-training centres, and many surrounded by village schools, have been built. In reality, these institutions of healing and enlightenment form active and enduring evidence of his influence in many areas. As he foresaw, the teaching of all schools and the industrial and health development they inculcated would eventually lead to the progress of the people towards civilization, however many the setbacks and delays encountered.

While the Treaty of 1873 helped to end the long-drawn-out campaign to stop the slave traffic, it only began the era of mission penetration and civilization. "This continent," he said, "must be civilized from within outwards." In other words, Africa must largely work out its own salvation—a prophetic forecast in view of the events of the last decade.

Livingstone's influence on his contemporaries was very great, placing him on the crest of a tremendous wave of public enthusiasm. Long before Lugard's day he was the mentor of the Colonial and Foreign Offices on all matters affecting tropical Africa. His efforts as a London Missionary Society missionary, 1841/1852, and as Leader of the Crusade against the Slave Trade, 1852/73, were crowned by his burial in Westminster Abbey, a unique honour made possible by the devotion of his "faithful few".

---

*The *Punch* cartoon of 1875 (p. 92) well illustrates how Arab-vested interests in Zanzibar were still strong enough to enable slave-carrying dhows to break the Treaty of 1873. In referring to his "conservatism" the Sultan cynically indicated how difficult was the task of the British Navy. In fact, naval action proved wholly inadequate, and very costly both in lives and money. In 1883, H.M.S. *London* and her fleet of small vessels were withdrawn. British and other war vessels continued to capture slave dhows. As late as 1898 a German vessel landed several hundred freed slaves at East London. These found refuge on Cape Mission stations; one of them (a Galla) was still at Lovedale in 1937— a link with the long-drawn-out campaign begun by Livingstone.

David Livingstone: Chronology

PROF. J. DESMOND CLARK and GERVAS CLAY

In 1955 a catalogue was produced for the exhibition of Livingstone relics, which was held in the town of Livingstone to celebrate the centenary of the discovery of the Victoria Falls by David Livingstone. For this catalogue a chronology of the main dates of Livingstone's life was prepared, the principal source of information being the biography of David Livingstone by Blaikie, which was at that time the fullest and most authoritative biography in existence. Since that date many new biographies have been published and so have part of the private journals and letters of David Livingstone. In the Rhodes-Livingstone Museum it is frequently necessary to reply to questions concerning the life of David Livingstone and the chronology given in the catalogue was often consulted. It became apparent that there were errors in this chronology, which has now been corrected and brought up to date.

When David Livingstone crossed Africa from the west coast to the east coast he was four days out in his reckoning when he arrived at the east coast. During his last journeys he was thirteen days out when he met Stanley so that the date given by him for his meeting with Stanley at Ujiji differs from that given by Stanley.

Since the first chronology was published the actual date on which David Livingstone discovered the Falls (16th November, 1855) has been found in one of his notebooks in his own handwriting, and this has solved a much debated question. It is, of course, possible that Livingstone was out in his reckoning at that time, but this we shall never know. In reprinting the chronology, corrected in accordance with the latest information, the dates given by Blaikie and by Seaver in his biography have been compared and where they agreed the date has been accepted, where they differ, other authorities have been consulted and the best evidence has been accepted.

It may be of interest to quote one or two instances of different dates recorded in different books. In Livingstone's *Missionary Travels* he states that he discovered the upper Zambesi at Sesheke at the end of June, whereas in his *Private Journals*, edited by Professor Schapera, the date is given as 4th August. Blaikie gives the date as 3rd August and Seaver as 4th August. The best evidence must be the *Private Journals* and the date of 4th August is therefore accepted.

The date given for the second ascent of the Shire and the discovery of Lake Shirwa is given by Seaver as April, 1859, by Blaikie as May, 1859, and by Professor Wallis as April, 1859, with the discovery of Lake Shirwa on 18th April.

The return to Bambarre in Manyuema country is given by Blaikie as 21st September and by Seaver and Wallis as 22nd July—the latter date is accepted.

Other discrepancies are of lesser importance, although it should be mentioned that Livingstone's second visit to the Victoria Falls in 1860 is recorded in his own *Narrative* as being 9th August, whereas Seaver gives it as 8th August. There seems no reason to doubt that 9th August is the correct date.

We are greatly indebted to the staff of the National Archives of Rhodesia and Nyasaland in Salisbury, who have checked our chronology against their own and have agreed with the validity of the chronology given here.

1813 March 19th	David Livingstone born in Blantyre, Lanarkshire. Seaver, 14.
1823	Began work as a piecer and subsequently spinner at the Blantyre Cotton Mills. Seaver, 17.
1836	Entered Anderson's College, Glasgow University to study medicine and theology. Seaver, 24.
1838 September 5th	Accepted as a missionary by the London Missionary Society. Seaver, 26.
1839 or 1840	Meeting with Dr Moffat of Kuruman and decision to work in Africa. Seaver, 31.
1840	Attends medical lectures in Charing Cross Hospital, London. Seaver, 32.
1840 November	Takes medical degree—Licentiate of the Faculty of Physicians and Surgeons, Glasgow University. Seaver, 37.
1840 November 20th	Ordained a missionary at Albion Street Chapel, London. Seaver, 39.
1840 December 8th	Sailed on the barque *George* for the Cape via Rio de Janeiro. Seaver, 39.
1841	Training in the use of the quadrant under Captain Donaldson. Seaver, 39.
1841 March 14th	Arrived at the Cape and thence to Algoa Bay, May 19th. Seaver, 42.
1841 July 31st	Arrived at Kuruman and before end of year carried out with Edwards a 700-mile exploratory journey among the Bechuana. Seaver, 47.

1842 February 10th	Set out on second journey among the Bechuana and returned in June. Seaver, 54 and 60.
1843 February 21st	Set out on journey to meet Sechele, chief of the Bakwena. Seaver, 63.
1843 June	Livingstone received permission from the London Missionary Society to found a mission to the north of Kuruman. Letter of 29.1.43. Seaver, 70.
1843 August	Set out with Edwards to reconnoitre site for mission at Mabotsa among the Bakatla, 250 miles north of Kuruman. Seaver, 75.
1843 August 28th	Chief of the Bakatla granted land at Mabotsa for mission purposes. Schapera. Missionary Correspondence, 50–1.
1843 December	Mission established at Mabotsa. Seaver, 78.
1844 February 16th	Mauled by wounded lion the injuries leaving him with a permanently shortened left arm. Seaver, 78.
1845 January 2nd	Married Mary Moffat, eldest daughter of Dr Robert Moffat and lived at Mabotsa. Seaver, 90.
1846	Removed to found Chonuane Mission forty miles north of Mabotsa in Chief Sechele's country. Seaver, 95.
1846–7	Two journeys eastward among the eastern Bechuana and to contact the Boers trekking north and west. Seaver, 99.

1847 August	Moved the mission to Kolobeng. Seaver, 104.
1848 October 1st	Sechele baptised at Kolobeng. Seaver, 107.
1849 June 1st	Journey into the Kalahari with Oswell and Murray to discover Lake Ngami. Seaver, 118.
1849 August 1st	Discovered Lake Ngami. Seaver, 122.
1850 April 26th	Departure, with his wife and children, from Kolobeng in what proved to be unsuccessful attempt to reach Sebituane and Makololo. Seaver, 126.
1851 April 24th	Trekked north with his family and Oswell across the Kalahari. Seaver, 134.
1851 June 21st	Met Sebituane. Seaver, 136.
1851 August 4th	Discovery of the Upper Zambesi. Reached Sesheke. Schapera. *Private Journals*, 38.
1852 March 16th	Arrived back in Cape Town. Studied under the Astronomer Royal, Sir Thomas Maclear. Seaver, 146.
1852 April 23rd	His family left for England. Seaver, 147.
1852 June 8th	Left Cape on return to Kolobeng. Seaver, 152.
1852 August 27th	Reached Kuruman. Kolobeng raided and burnt by a Boer Commando. Seaver, 153.
1852 December 14th	Set out to visit Sekeletu (Sebituane's successor) with a view to choosing suitable mission site in Barotseland. Seaver, 166.

1853 May 23rd	Arrived at Linyanti. Schapera. *Private Journals*, 137.
1853	Journey through the Barotse Valley. Seaver, 181.
1853 November 11th	Left Linyanti for the west coast. Seaver, 187.
1854 May 31st	Arrived at St. Paul do Loanda, capital of Angola. Seaver, 218.
1854 September 20th	Set off on return journey to the east coast. Seaver, 223.
1855 September 10th	Returned to Linyanti on the Chobe. Seaver, 244.
1855 November 3rd	Left Linyanti for Quelimane. Seaver, 249.
1855 November 16th	Discovered the Victoria Falls. Notebook in Museum.
1855 December 18th	Discovered the Kafue River. Seaver, 254.
1856 May 20th	Reached the east coast at Qualimane. Seaver, 264.
1856 July 12th	Sailed for England via Mauritius. Seaver, 274.
1856 December 9th	Returned to England. Seaver, 276.
1857	*Missionary Travels* published. Many honours conferred upon him. Resigned from the London Missionary Society. Seaver, 282–3.
1857 December 4th	Cambridge Lectures which led to the founding of the Universities Mission on November 1st, 1858. Seaver, 291.
1858 February 8th	Appointed Her Majesty's Consul at Quelimane for the eastern coast and

	independent districts of the interior and commander of an expedition for exploring eastern and central Africa. Seaver, 308.
1858 March 12th	Sailed with his family and the members of the Zambesi Expedition in the steamer *Pearl* for the Cape. Wallis. Zambesi Expedition 1.
1858 May 14th	Zambesi Expedition arrived at the mouth of the Zambesi. Seaver, 322.
1858 May 19th	Proceeded up river in the *Ma-Robert*. Wallis, Vol, I, p. 7.
1858 November 8th to 13th	Discovery of the impassable barrier of the Kebrabasa Rapids. Seaver, 332.
1859 January	Exploration of the Shire River. Seaver, 339.
1859 April 18th	Second ascent of the Shire and discovery of Lake Shirwa. Wallis, 316.
1859 August	Third journey up the Shire. Seaver, 350.
1859 September 17th	Re-discovery of Lake Nyasa. Seaver, 350.
1860	Journey with his brother and Dr Kirk to the Upper Zambesi. Seaver, 365.
1860 August 9th	Second visit to the Victoria Falls. Livingstone *Narrative*, 250.
1860 September 17th	Return journey from Sesheke to Tete arriving November 23rd. Seaver, 377 and 381.
1861 January 31st	Arrival of the *Pioneer* with Bishop Mackenzie and the members of the Universities Mission to Central Africa. Livingstone *Narrative*, 348.

The front and back of a medal awarded to 60 of Livingstone's followers by the Royal Geographical Society, 1874.

The Last Mile.

MORE SLAVERIES THAN ONE.

RIGHT HON. B. D. "Now that your Highness has seen the blessings of Freedom, I trust we may rely upon your strenuous help in putting down Slavery?"

SULTAN SEYYID BARGHASH. "Ah, yes! Certainly! But remember, O SHEIKH BEN DIZZY, CONSERVATIVE PARTY VERY STRONG in Zanzibar!"

Engraving showing a British cruiser chasing slave dhows and in the foreground a cutter crossing bar to rescue survivors from beached dhow.

1861 February 25th	Commencement of the first unsuccessful attempt to explore the Rovuma River. *Narrative*, 349.
1861 July	Mission party settled at Magomero in Southern Nyasaland. Seaver, 391.
1861 September 2nd	Exploration of Lake Nyasa commenced. Seaver, 395.
1862 January 31st	*Lady Nyassa* delivered in sections by H.M.S. *Gorgon* at the mouth of the Zambesi. Mrs Livingstone and additional mission party arrive. Seaver, 405.
1862 January 31st	Death of Bishop Mackenzie. Seaver, 405.
1862 April 27th	Death of Mrs Livingstone at Shupanga. Seaver, 411.
1862 June 23rd	Launching of the *Lady Nyassa*. *Narrative*, 423.
1862 September 9th	Exploration of the Rovuma River commenced. Seaver, 416.
1863 January	Return to the Zambesi and commencement of the fourth journey to Lake Nyasa with the intention of launching the *Lady Nyassa* there. Seaver, 422.
1863 July 2nd	Received despatch from Earl Russell recalling the expedition. Livingstone *Narrative*, 471.
1864 February 14th	Sailed the *Lady Nyassa* from Quelimane via Mozambique and Zanzibar to Bombay. Livingstone *Narrative*, 578.
1864 June 13th	Arrived in Bombay. Seaver, 449.

1864 July 23rd	Arrived in London. Seaver, 452.
1864 September 19th	Address to the British Association at Bath concerning the slave trade. Seaver, 456.
1864 September 26th —April 25th	At Newstead Abbey writing his book, *Narrative of a Expedition to the Zambesi and its Tributaries: and of the Discovery of Lakes Shirwa and Nyassa.* Blaikie, 291 to 297.
1865 August	Sailed again for Africa via Bombay. Seaver, 469.
1866 January 28th	Arrived at Zanzibar. Seaver, 474.
1866 March 19th	Left Zanzibar for mouth of Rovuma. Seaver, 481.
1866 August 8th	Reached Lake Nyasa and crossed to south end of lake. Seaver, 492.
1866 December	False report of his death reached Zanzibar. Blaikie, 318.
1866 December 15th	Crossed the Luangwa Valley to Lake Tanganyika. Waller, Vol. II, p. 159.
1867 April 2nd	Reached south end of Lake Tanganyika. Seaver, 510.
1867 July 25th	Livingstone Search Expedition under the command of Lieut E. D. Young arrived at mouth of Zambezi and proceeded to refute story of Livingstone's death. Young, 59. (*In Search of Livingstone.*)
1867 November 8th	Discovered Lake Mweru. Scarcity of provisions. Befriended by Arab Mohamad Bogharib. Visited Chief Kasembe and explored the Luapula Valley. Seaver, 515 to 516.

1868 July 18th	Discovered Lake Bangweulu. Seaver, 524.
1868 December 11th	Joined party of Arabs to return to Ujiji. Blaikie, 326.
1869 March 14th	Reached Ujiji on eastern shore of Lake Tanganyika. Seaver, 534.
1869 July 12th	Set out to explore the Manyuema country and Lualaba River to north-west of the lake. Seaver, 539.
1870 July 22nd	Returned to Bambarre in Manyuema country and remained there in poor health. Waller. *Last Journal*, Vol II, 47.
1871 February 16th	Left Bambarre to explore Lualaba. Seaver, 555.
1871 March 29th	Reached Nyangwe on Lualaba, fur-thest westward point reached by him on last expedition. Seaver, 559.
1871 July 15th	Massacre by Arab slavers on Lualaba witnessed. Seaver, 566.
1871 July 20th	Began return journey to Ujiji. Seaver, 570.
1871 August 8th	Escaped ambush. Seaver, 570.
1871 November 5th	Reached Ujiji greatly exhausted. (Re-corded by Livingstone as October 23rd, as he was thirteen days out in his reckoning.) Seaver, 573.
1871 November 10th	Met by H. M. Stanley who had been sent to Africa to look for him by the *New York Herald*. (Recorded by Livingstone as October 28th, as he was thirteen days out in his reckon-ing.) Seaver, 574 and 579.

1871	Journey with Stanley to north end of lake. Seaver, 585.
1871 December 27th	Set out for Unyanyembe* with Stanley. Blaikie, 360.
1872 March 14th	Parted with Stanley at Unyanyembe. Stanley started on return journey to Zanzibar. Seaver, 595.
1872 August 25th	Left Unyanyembe to return to Lake Tanganyika. Seaver, 611.
1872	Journeyed down east side of lake. Seaver, 611.
1873 January	Approached Lake Bangweulu, this time from north-east side. Seaver, 616.
1873 April	Became seriously ill. Last days of travel. Seaver, 622.
1873 May 1st	Died in Chitambo's Village, Ilala. Seaver, 627.
1874 February	Livingstone's followers reached Bagamoyo after having carried his body and possessions 2 000 miles to the coast. Waller, 344.
1874 April 18th	Buried with national honours in Westminster Abbey. Macnair, 402.
1874 November	Publication of *The Last Journals of David Livingstone*. Waller.

BIBLIOGRAPHY
1. BLAIKIE, WILLIAM GARDEN. *The Personal Life of David Livingstone*. 6th Ed.: 1913. John Murray, London.
2. LIVINGSTONE, DAVID AND CHARLES. *Narrative of an Expedition to the Zambesi and its Tributaries.* 1858–1864. 1865. John Murray, London.

3. LIVINGSTONE, DAVID. Original Notebook in Rhodes-Livingstone Museum, Livingstone, Northern Rhodesia.

4. MACNAIR, DR JAMES, I. *Livingstone's Travels*. 1954. J. M. Dent and Sons, London.

5. SCHAPERA, I. (Ed.). *Livingstone's Private Journals*. 1851–1853. 1960. Chatto and Windus, London.

6. SEAVER, GEORGE. *David Livingstone. His Life and Times*. 1957. Lutterworth Press, London.

7. WALLER, DR HORACE. *The Last Journals of David Livingstone*. 1874. John Murray, London.

8. WALLIS, J. P. R. (Ed.). *The Zambesi Expedition of David Livingstone*, 1858–1863. 1956. Chatto and Windus, London.

9. YOUNG, LIEUT E. D. *In Search of Livingstone*. 1868. Letts and Co.

BRIEF BIOGRAPHICAL DATA ON CONTRIBUTORS

1. ATKINSON, NORMAN, D.Litt., Ph.D. Trinity College, Dublin; Senior lecturer in Education, University of Rhodesia, since 1968. Author of "History of Irish Education", "Educating the African—Rhodesia" (1972) and "History of Commonwealth Education" (1973).

2. BRADLOW, FRANK R., F.R.G.S., B.Comm. (Wits.), A.C.I.S. Chairman, Friends of the South African Library, of which he is a Trustee: Co-author with his wife, Edna, of "Thomas Bowler: his Life and Work", and several other Africana, including a forthcoming on life of Thomas Baines. War Service, World War II, wounded. Besides his multifarious business interests, he finds time to collect Africana and became expert in many of its aspects, particularly on South African painters and their works.

3. CLARK, Prof. J. DESMOND, Prof. of Anthropology, Univ. of California since 1961. Ph.D. Cantab, 1950; Research in Northern Rhodesia 1938-1961. Military service 1941-46. Many publications on pre-history and archaeology in Africa. Author of Rhodes-Livingstone Exhibition Catalogue 1955 and many articles in Northern Rhodesia Journal, including Chronology done with Gervas Clay.

4. CLAY, GERVAS, C.R. of Lancing College, Oxford; Cadet Northern Rhodesia 1930; D.O. 1932. Author of papers in the Northern Rhodesia Journal. Married daughter of Lord Baden-Powell.

5. GELFAND, MICHAEL, Prof. C.B.E., M.D., F.R.C.P. Professor of Medicine, University of Rhodesia. Resident in Rhodesia since 1936; has made extensive researches into Shona Religion and Customs. Author of thirty books, mostly of African interest, including "Livingstone the Doctor", 1957. Physician to the Royal Family while in Rhodesia.

6. GLUCKMAN, MAX, M.A., D.Phil. (Oxon.). Professor of Social Anthropology in the Victoria Manchester University since 1949. Over twenty years research in Africa. Author of some twenty books on African Anthropology, Broadcaster and visiting lecturer in United Kingdom and America. Lives in Cheshire; is one of the leading authorities on African culture and political evolution.

7. KEYNES, QUENTIN. Great-grandson of Charles Darwin; world traveller and photographer. Author of many travel articles, including one on recent visit to Galapagos Islands to film giant tortoises; when not in Africa on annual safaris, lives either in London or New York. Owns collection of rare Livingstone items recently used by B.B.C. for their centenary film (1973).

8. LLOYD, GERAINT OWEN, B.A., son of the Rev A. Lloyd of Swellendam and Paarl. For two generations, since 1912, the Lloyds of Paarl have minis-

tered to Congregational churches in Southern Africa. The Rev. G.O. does so now in Salisbury. He writes on the "Livingstone Legend" with almost 40 years' experience of mission and church work. He studied at Livingstone College, Leyton.

9. LLOYD, BRENDAN W., M.A., T.C. Dublin. Lived (1931–37) in South Africa and in Rhodesia since 1937, as teacher of History and as African Schools Inspector. 1939–44 War Service; 1945 Headmaster in Addis Ababa for British Council. Africana collector and author of monograph "Men of Livingstone" and editor of this Symposium and a bibliography of Livingstone. Born Dublin (1904); lives in Rhodesia.

10. PACHAI, BRIDGLAL, M.A., Ph.D. Professor of History, Univ. of Malawi, born in South Africa; worked in University of Cape Coast, Ghana; widely travelled in Europe, the U.S.A., Africa and India. Author of six books on African history including "Malawi Past and Present" (1972) and "Livingstone; Man of Africa Memorial Essays, 1873–1973".

By a strip of land only five or six miles wide, and as we subsequently discovered, a prolongation of the Shirwa Lake, some 30 miles south of the point we reached (15° 23') is about 30 miles distant from a branch of the Shire up which we went in this vessel 7 or 8 miles — The Lake Shirwa is about 25 or 30 miles wide and probably sixty or seventy long — is situated in a beautiful highland region the mountains being over 6000 feet high — This does not seem to be the "Lake Maravi" of the Maps, for there are no Maravi near. The Portuguese know nothing about it, and we deem it right to say little about it tile it is divulged to them by our own Government.